GETTING INVOLVED WITH YOUR OWN COMPUTER

A Guide for Beginners

LESLIE SOLOMON
STANLEY VEIT

RIDLEY ENSLOW PUBLISHERS

60 Crescent Place, Box 301
Short Hills, New Jersey 07078

Library of Congress Cataloging in Publication Data

Solomon, Leslie.
Getting involved with your own computer.

1. Microcomputers. I Veit, Stanley, joint author. II. Title.

QA76.5.S6533 001.6'4'04 77-8498
ISBN 0-89490-003-X
ISBN 0-89490-004-8 pbk.

Printed in the United States of America

10 9 8 7 6 5 4 3

GETTING INVOLVED WITH YOUR OWN COMPUTER

To

Bev and Dede

Contents

Figures

Photographs

GETTING INVOLVED WITH YOUR OWN COMPUTER

1 Introduction

It all started with the fingers. Because that was all early man had to keep track of events that interested him, we can honestly say that it all started digitally!

Then came the transition from fingers to pebbles, stones, and small pieces of wood or bone, and man had invested the new science of "keeping tabs on things," now called "data processing."

At some time in those early days man learned to make marks on soft stone, bits of wood, or semihardened mud, and a written language was born; most likely the first writing represented some form of number.

The first counting "machine" was developed by an unknown mathematician (perhaps a trader who wanted to keep accurate records) about 2000 years ago. Although it is known by many names, we still recognize it as the abacus, a mathematical machine used to this day in Asia and often displayed in shops alongside its twentieth-century counterpart, the electronic calculator. Despite the antiquity of the abacus, a skillful operator can add, subtract, multiply, and divide at speeds rivaling modern calculators. Its basic operation is described in Appendix A.

In 1643 Blaise Pascal developed his arithmetic machine, an ingenious device operated by a series of wheels and on which the digits 0 through 9 were scribed around its perimeter. A small tab on the edge of the wheel near the number 9 formed the "carry." By entering a number on the right-hand wheel and passing 9 the carry tab caused the next adjacent wheel to rotate to the 1 position (to form 10). This same principle is used today in the automobile odometer which indicates how many miles a car has traveled. The electronic version of Pascal's idea can be found in the "carry" output of an electronic digital decade counter.

In 1694 Leibnitz' modification of Pascal's arithmetic machine could produce direct multiplications and division. This conversion remained in use for many years, for it wasn't until 1834 that the first major change occurred. In that year Charles Babbage designed his "analytic engine," which incorporated instructions on a punched card, a main feature of modern digital computers. Although Babbage envisioned memory and output devices, they were still far in the future.

The punched-card approach was reexamined by Herman Hollerith in 1890, at which time electromechanical devices had already been made available by the fledgling science of electricity. Hollerith punched holes in a card to represent the letters of the alphabet and the digits 0 through 9. The code he developed, the Hollerith 80-column punch card code, is still in use today.

It is interesting to note that the Hollerith card reader worked much like a modern paper-tape reader. A series of metal pins placed in contact with a card touched a pool of mercury under the card whenever its perforations allowed the pins to pass through. When contact was made, an electric circuit was completed. Wherever there were no holes, no closed circuit was made.

The Hollerith approach was used to "computerize" the 1890 Census by classifying the population by name, address, sex, and other pertinent data, according to the holes punched in the cards; it took only one-third the time required by the Census of 1880.

The punched card method was subsequently adopted by the government for other uses and a new industry was born. In 1911 the manufacturer of Hollerith's equipment merged with another company to form the organization now known as International Business Machines (IBM).

The electromechanical calculating engine was constantly improved, and in 1885 the Burroughs adding machine appeared, followed in 1917 by the introduction of the first calculator to perform multiplication, division, addition, and subtraction. During World War I these primitive computers formed the first fire-control system for artillery batteries.

In 1944 Howard Aiken of Harvard designed the MARK 1, the first of the large digital computers, which, once its program had been installed, could perform all operations without the assistance of a human operator. This large (5-ton) device used 3304 electromechanical relays for its memory. The MARK 1 was retired in 1959. Some of its parts are on display at Harvard and at the Smithsonian Institution in Washington.

About the same time Aiken was working on the MARK 1 George Stibitz of Bell Laboratories designed and built the Bell Model-1 which set a record for reliability; it could be left running overnight without an operator in attendance.

Electronics entered the picture in 1946 when ENIAC was built, using vacuum tube logic. Mauchly and Eckert, the inventors of ENIAC, faced the problem of unreliable vacuum tubes. The 18,000 tubes required by ENIAC had an expected failure rate of one every 7 1/2 minutes!

Special vacuum tubes were invented to provide increased reliability, and soon ENIAC could operate for several days at a time without tube failure.

A giant step in computer design was made in 1946 when John Von Neumann proposed that both operating instructions and data be stored in the machine's memory. The first of the new devices built in accordance with this proposal was the EDSAC, installed at the University of Cambridge in 1949. It was also this idea, built into the MANIAC, that helped the United States to produce the H-bomb.

The transistor, forerunner in the semiconductor industry, was designed more than 25 years ago at Bell Laboratories. In the last 15 years, however, a new concept has been applied: the semiconductor integrated circuit (IC). This novel device, an offspring of the process that introduced the first transistor, allows dozens, then hundreds, then thousands of transistors to be built up in a small piece of silicon. Called diffusion technique, it was adapted to the manufacture of complex integrated circuits for counting, latching, and conversion in usable form by operating readout devices such as seven-segment gas tubes or solid-state devices like the seven-segment LEDs (light-emitting diodes) and liquid crystals.

As more was learned about digital logic and diffusion techniques were improved, large-scale integrated circuits (LSI) were designed in which not only new forms of low-power transistor were used but passive elements such as resistors and capacitors could be created.

Once LSI devices became practical, the pocket calculator was marketed. A look around most shops will show the present state of the art.

Electronic calculators were improved so rapidly that even the small ones could store some memory, perform complex operations, and sometimes print the answers. Only a few years ago someone came up with the idea of mating the older computer technology with the all-electronics approach, with the result that when the computer logic was given instructions the arithmetic portion could operate on them and deliver a usable output. The entire logic and arithmetic circuit was then built into one chip and the microprocessor (computer-on-a-chip) made its appearance.

The first of these microprocessors was a logical extension of the scientific calculators, and it didn't take long for semiconductor manufacturers to realize they had a tiger by the tail. Development followed development, until many different types of microprocessor were made available to customers who understood how to use them. The original cost was high; only three or four years ago the 8080 was priced at $300. Today it can be bought for less than $20.

The high cost of processors kept them out of the hands of the then small band of computer hobbyists, who were mostly programmers and engineers who could operate only by sneaking time on their company computers or by trying to reactivate old junked equipment. They longed for their own machines.

In the mid-70s Intel introduced its 8008 microprocessor, which had little more power than a good scientific calculator, but only a few hobbyists showed interest. It was the 8080, Intel's new and more powerful chip, that was destined to revolutionize small computers. In the January 1975 issue of *Popular Electronics* an article described the construction of the relatively low-cost Altair computer, which is based on the 8080. That introduction was the beginning of the present wave of hobby computers.

Since that time the cost of the 8080 microprocessor chip has dropped to less than $20. Now there are many different microprocessors and each has its own adherents. There is no "best" design; each hobbyist must decide which he prefers after reading about them and talking to his friends.

Since the introduction of the first hobby, or personal, computer there has been a literal explosion of peripherals (external devices) to go with each computer. The variety of these low-cost peripherals has amazed even the computer professionals. It is now possible to get just about every imaginable adjunct to a personal computer, including a vocal input and a color graphic system, all at a reasonable price. A glance at any of the hobby magazines will show what is currently available and the end is not yet in sight.

USES OF A PERSONAL COMPUTER

Thousands of applications can be found for the personal computer in homes, businesses, schools, laboratories, and entertainment. Following are just a few of the uses to which people are putting them. A further discussion of applications appears in Chapter 13.

In the Home

A computer can provide a home accounting system for family control of income and expenditures. This includes such items as balancing the checkbook and calculating the taxes.

It can provide an on-going inventory of family possessions for insurance purposes. The list can be updated with each purchase.

It can control the "automatic house" by programming appliances to start and stop as required.

It can control automatic garden watering and lighting systems that take both weather and soil conditions into account.

It can provide a home security system that can be programmed to warn of intruders, fire, smoke, or heating and appliance failures.

It can monitor the house, itself, with fire and smoke detectors, intrusion alarms, climate control devices, and even warn of water seepage in the basement.

A computer can also provide home secretarial service by keeping track of family members and their schedules. It can take and deliver messages by print-out and it can receive or originate telephone calls.

Entertainment Applications

The personal computer can play thousands of games that are educational as well as fun. The hobbyist can control a space ship landing on a far planet; he can be the ruler of an empire, captain of a warship or of the Star Ship *Enterprise* on a voyage of exploration to the ends of the known universe; or he can match wits with a computer in games of chess, backgammon, or Go.

The personal computer has made possible a new type of game that involves the control of patterns and colors with a "joystick" and color TV.

Educational Applications

The personal computer has vast potential as an educational tool. Educators in increasing numbers are buying them to introduce computerized instruction into the classroom at reasonable cost. The current budget crunch in the schools has compelled conversion from the larger and more expensive computers to the new and smaller designs. This use of microcomputers will mean that the next generation will grow up with computers and will be able to understand and control them.

Scientific Applications

Science and research are the sum of many observations. Laboratories in research departments are finding that small computers are ideal for recording data and controlling experiments. In addition, many experiments can be simplified by computer simulation. This frees dollars and people for more creative activities.

CHOOSING YOUR PERSONAL COMPUTER

Because the initial investment in a computer system will be relatively large, any person thinking about buying one should be careful that the equipment purchased will fit into his concept of a system. The high cost precludes changing systems in midstream. Bear in mind that whatever is selected will be obsolete in terms of the latest on the market. This does not matter if the equipment does the job it was meant to do. Large computers built 10 years ago are still doing the work they have always done, despite the fact that by today's standards they have been long out of date. As new machines come on line the prices of the older ones go down. Thus they are made available to users who could not buy them at the original price. We are all working with "used computers"; perhaps you, too, can save money by buying out-of-date equipment. Be careful, however; you can buy a machine with problems because of poor maintenance. Do not buy unless you can get a guarantee from the seller that he can fix the machine and will be there when you need him.

This book presents the facts about the choice of a personal computer and its use. It cannot, of course, cover developments after its publication, but the general information presented will apply to most machines in the near future.

A few years ago small computers did not exist; today they are moving into the lives of everyone. No one can quite predict the changes they will cause or the form they will take. This book describes what is here now and provides a glimpse of the future.

2 Where Can You Find Out About Personal Computers?

Researching the personal computer field is almost a hobby in itself. Once bitten by the computer bug, most hobbyists spend a lot of time and money reading and attending show and club meetings to learn more about computers and software. The big question is "What kind of a system shall I buy?" A lot of help is available to answer this question and this chapter is intended to tell you where to find it.

MAGAZINES

The idea of constructing a computer or video terminal at home was first brought to the attention of the general public by *Popu-*

lar Electronics and *Radio Electronics.* With this initial public awareness as a springboard, the publication of *BYTE* encouraged the personal computer explosion and its success led to the introduction of other magazines. Eight of nine are now devoted to personal computing and considerable coverage is supplied by the "big" computer publications.

In addition, each of the clubs publishes a newsletter, some of which contain information on construction, software, and new products. Because these clubs exchange information, much of value is constantly being reprinted all over the country.

The leading magazines can be obtained at computer stores or by subscription. The following is a list of periodicals currently available.

BYTE

BYTE is the largest and most popular magazine in the field at this time. *BYTE* magazine grew out of a small, self-published technical newsletter created by Carl Helmers in 1974. It is sold by subscription and on the racks of local computer stores. Each issue contains valuable features and old issues are prized as much as the current one! This "back issue mania" applies to many hobbyist publications. It is not unusual to find the current issue and as many back issues as the store has been able to obtain for sale on the same rack. *BYTE* is published by BYTE Publications, 70 Main Street, Peterborough, N. H. 03458. If you subscribe, allow about six weeks for your order to be processed.

Microcomputer SCCS Interface

Microcomputer SCCS Interface is a publication of the Southern California Computer Society, which has developed into a national computer hobbyist's organization. It contains much of interest to hobbyists all over the world and is staffed by leaders in the field. The magazine is distributed to members. Apply to the Southern California Computer Society, P.O. Box 60114, Terminal Annex, Los Angeles, Calif. 90060.

Interface Age

This magazine split off from the older publication *Microcomputer SCCS Interface*. It is a product of the commercial publishers who produced *Microcomputer SCCS Interface* for the Society. It is an excellent magazine and carries many articles of interest and a lot of free software. Subscriptions to *Interface Age* can be obtained from *Interface Age,* P.O. Box 1234, Cerritos, Calif. 90701.

KILOBAUD

This magazine is the current publication of Wayne Green. It first appeared in January 1977 and quickly became one of the leading publications in the field. It costs a little more than some of the other magazines but its pages are crammed with important articles and features. The staff has been able to maintain a balance between hardware and software articles and most hobbyists are eager to read it. *KILOBAUD* is sold in computer stores and is obtainable by subscription from *KILOBAUD,* Peterborough, N.H. 03458.

Don't be surprised if back issues are priced higher than new issues! The older the issue, the scarcer it has become, and the more valuable it may be!

73

This Wayne Green publication is devoted to ham radio, but it also contains a section called I/O which supplies technical information on computers. It specializes in construction articles popular with the do-it-yourself addicts.

Creative Computing

This bimonthly magazine was one of the first devoted to the noncommercial uses of computers. It is addressed to educational computing and to applications in the visual arts, music, and games. David Ahl, the dynamic publisher of *Creative Computing,* has promoted computers in the schools and the arts in articles, at shows and conventions, and by sending copies of the magazine to educational institutions.

Since the explosion of the personal computer hobby this magazine has supplied both hardware and software coverage of personal computing and reviews of books on the subject. For those who want to acquire something more than technical knowledge *Creative Computing* is ideal. It is sold in computer stores and by subscription from *Creative Computing,* P.O. Box 789-M, Morristown, N.J. 07960.

ROM

The newest entry on the magazine list for personal computer hobbyists is aimed at the users of the next generation of personal computers. It features articles on the uses of the new complete systems computers rather than on the hobbyist who builds equipment and programs in machine language. Because this group is increasing as fast as the ready-built computers appear on the market at lower cost, *ROM* will be popular with a lot of people. In computerese ROM means "Read-Only-Memory," a term for memory chips with a "burned-in" program; this magazine title, however, means "Read-Only-Magazine," which implies that the hobbyist will find both ideas and programs between its covers. *ROM* is sold in computer and general magazine stores and is available by subscription from ROM Publications Corp., Route 97, Hampton, Conn. 06247.

Personal Computing

Personal Computing is a somewhat different magazine in that it addresses the entire field, which constitutes those who use time sharing or school computers and those who are just interested in reading about them. This readership is certain to include the group of users of ready-built machines just now appearing on the market. Subscriptions may be obtained from *Personal Computing,* Benwell Publishing Corp., 167 Corey Road, Brookline Mass. 02146.

Dr. Dobbs Journal of Computer Calisthenics and Orthodontia—Running Light Without OverByte

This rather fancifully titled magazine is really *The Journal of Free Software,* and because it carries no ads it gives its opinions of hardware and the practices of manufacturers and retailers. This excellent publication is the product of The People's Computer Co., an educational nonprofit organization devoted to computer instruction for just about anybody, but especially the kids. PCC also publishes a newspaper called *People's Computer.* Both publications are available from DDJ, 1010 Dole, P.O. Box E, Menlo Park, Calif. 94025.

Popular Electronics

This general electronics magazine, although not devoted solely to personal computing, has been in the forefront of microcomputer development. The Altair first appeared in its pages as a construction project, as did the COSMAC Elf. Most hobbyists read *Popular Electronics* for new ideas and for its monthly computer column.

Radio Electronics

This general circulation magazine also features computer construction projects and a monthly hobby computer column.

Electronic Design, EDN, Datamation

These limited circulation magazines are available only to the computer and electronics industries. They often contain valuable information for anyone concerned with microprocessors.

EDN has now made it a practice to send back issues to some of the computer stores for distribution to students who have been unable to obtain free subscriptions. It is hoped that other magazines with limited circulation will take up this idea.

BOOKS

The lists of many publishers of technical books contain simple introductions to highly technical texts on microcomputers and the microcomputer explosion. The new hobbyist seeking information can browse among them in the local computer store or book shop. Most of the magazines feature book reviews of new titles and the publishers' latest ads. *Creative Computing* has reviewed and classified books on BASIC language and other topics. It is therefore not difficult to find the best book on a subject of interest. In addition, several of the magazines sell books by mail. Many of the most interesting books in the field are published by independent publishers. Our book is in that category; another is Adam Osborn's *Introduction to Microprocessors. Bugbook,* vols. 1, 2, 2A, and 3, contains good training texts on digital logic and microprocessors, and *Computer Lib* by Ted Nelson is a classic.

The technical literature of semiconductor manufacturers includes manuals, specification sheets, application notes, and general educational material. Texas Instruments, Motorola, Intel, Mostek, and other chip makers offer excellent books at very low cost. Their lists are available on request and many of their publications can be obtained from computer stores or electronics distributors.

Books, manuals, and brochures are available from many manufacturers when the request is made on a corporate letterhead. They are also sent to experimenters who ask for them. Sometimes they are available at electronics parts distributors (check the yellow pages of your phone book).

Because of the laws that deny patent protection to software, but grant copyrights to books that contain it, many companies supply it in that form. The price of published software may be higher than usual book prices; however, you are paying for the labor of program development as well as the expense of publication. Hobby magazines carry ads for software and often feature articles on it.

Most computer hobbyists are avid readers and have extensive book collections. It is wise to read a great deal before investing in your personal computer.

CATALOGS

Most computer stores have catalogs that list the lines they sell and are glad to give them to anyone who is interested. Study various items in the magazines and ask for the specific ones you need.

If your local dealer cannot supply the brochure you want, write to the manufacturer for it. Occasionally you will be asked for a small fee to cover the costs of mailing. Sending for catalogs by mail will also give you some idea of the reaction time of the company you are planning to buy from. Read the catalogs carefully and pay attention to what they do *not* say as well as what they do. Do not assume that the merchandise described as "available soon," "under development," or "coming soon" will be there when you need it. Count on the items that are being shipped NOW. It is possible that those that were advertised at the time the brochure was written will never be produced. Be wary of delivery dates of new products. Many companies announce new products long in advance of the actual delivery date. Sometimes this is deliberate, but it can also be caused by the disruption of production schedules because of nondelivery of parts.

CLUBS

Your local computer club is one of the most reliable sources of information on personal computers. It is composed of people who have built equipment and know what each system is like. In addition, manufacturers and computer stores demonstrate new products at club meetings, distribute catalogs, and answer questions, and seminars are frequently held on one type of machine or another.

A word of warning about club members and computer hobbyists in general: they are very loyal to the type and brand of machine they own. You may get a distorted picture if you ask an Altair owner about an IMSAI and vice versa. Both will give you a negative view of the merits of the SWTPC 6800 and may scorn an unknown make! When a new product comes out, however, everyone shows an interest and some may try to encourage other club members to buy. Consider the newest machine with care. It may have all the features you think you want, but it is hard sometimes to be a pioneer—that is, the first kid on the block with a "superduper" new computer.

One more thing: a club is a source of help if you get into trouble with your first machine. A lot of experienced hobbyists are always ready to help a fellow member.

How do you find out where your local computer club is? Well, most of the magazines list them all. If there is none where you live, you can do one of two things: first, write a letter to the editors of some of the magazines and ask them to print your request that hobbyists in your area help you start a club. As an alternative you can join the Southern California Computer Society. This may sound funny if you live in Maine, but there are members all over the world. You could even form the Northern Maine chapter of the SCCS! There already is a Delaware chapter. The advantage is that you will become a member of an established group that produces a fine magazine, worth the price of membership alone. In addition, you get in on club group purchases and advice and help from special interest groups. Even if contact is by club mail, you can get help with your problems. Naturally, a local club is best, but it may be worth a trip to attend meetings.

School clubs are among those who offer young students an opportunity to learn computer languages and to operate machines. Many schools sponsor these clubs for their programs of instruction and time sharing on school or district computers. Under teacher supervision, members are permitted to develop their own programs. In addition, several clubs publish excellent magazines and serve as software exchanges. *Creative Computing Magazine* often prints news and lists of school clubs and conducts a national circulation forum for their ideas. *People's Computer* of Menlo Park, Calif., a newspaper of interest to students and leaders of educational computing clubs, is devoted to club news, software, and personal computing. The computer club idea started in California and has now spread across the United States and Canada.

With the development of the personal computer hobby, many clubs have raised money to buy microcomputer kits, and, directed by teachers, have built and operated club centers equipped with hobby-type computers. In many areas this has resulted in the expansion of school computing facilities, for clubs have been able to put the new machines to practical use.

As a measure of recognition the semiconductor manufacturers

are making available to schools at only the cost of distribution their microcomputer chip sets with minor cosmetic defects. Intel is one company that has promoted school interest in microcomputers. Clubs have also used these chip sets to give their members a chance to "home brew" their own computers and to learn how they work. Often the local adult computer club helps to form the school clubs and to construct the club computers.

COMPUTER STORES

The first computer store, which was given the original name, "The Computer Store," was opened in Los Angeles. This name is now popular with Altair dealers. The Computer Mart of New York was the first on the East Coast. In the last year many more have opened until today there are stores throughout the country.

Most computer shops sell a variety of brands and offer the new computerer a wide choice of products. Some are devoted to the Altair line and carry only those products that are not in competition with it. If both types of store are available to you, visit them and ask questions. The storekeeper is in business to help you and he will present his products as completely as possible to meet your demands. He wants you to buy and is counting on you as a customer now and in the future. Consider the products he sells on their merits; consider also the help he will give you to build a kit, repair a machine that "goes down," and to get software to run on your computer. Your computer store will provide all these aids to the enjoyment of your equipment. A characteristic of a good store is its ability to repair your equipment. No matter how well they are built, sooner or later all computers will need help. Your local shop is the most reliable place to get it. Unless your machine is under warranty, however, don't expect to get repair service for nothing. Repairs of microprocessor equipment are often time consuming and complex. Your dealer must at least break even on the repair work if he is to survive in business. You can still send your machine back to the manufacturer, but that takes a lot of time and he hasn't the same incentive to please you. For those who live where there are still no computer stores, many mail-order houses will sell you equipment and so will some manufacturers.

3 How to Communicate with a Computer

Being blessed with an active imagination, an intense curiosity regarding the world about him, and 10 discrete, readily available fingers, man has always found it easy to communicate "amounts" to other men, even those who spoke another language. As long as the number did not exceed 10 and both sides understood the system, all went well.

When calculating devices, such as the abacus, entered man's world a thousand or more years ago, new number systems had to be devised so that the machine could be given "amounts" with which to operate and produce a comprehensible result.

This led to some disagreement about what a "number system" is and how the same number could be expressed in different ways.

First, the concept of 0 (zero) had to be understood. Without delving into its history, all you have to keep in mind is that 0 is not nothing but a real live number. Consider the difference between $1 and $1,000,000 and you will appreciate the power of the zero. This zero concept meant that the old "count to 10 on the fingers" had to be reexamined.

NUMBERING SYSTEMS

Human beings have only 10 fingers, and if each finger is used only once the highest count that can be made is 9. Wait a minute, you may say . . . I always thought that I could count to 10 on my fingers. But the number 10 consists of *two* digits—a 1 and a 0. To illustrate the 0, which is a real and very important digit, we shall have to start the finger counting with 0. Now, if this is done, you will soon find out just how high you can count on only 10 fingers.

This means that in the decimal system to which we have become accustomed we have only the digits 0 through 9; the next count is the "carry." To illustrate the carry imagine two people, each with 10 fingers, holding both hands out with only one finger extended to indicate the zero of that set of digits. The first person (units) now extends a second finger to indicate 1, then another finger to indicate 2, until all fingers on both hands are extended to indicate a count of 9. At the next count, 10, the units per son closes one hand and four fingers on the other to indicate a zero; the second person (tens) extends a second finger to indicate a 1.

At this point the first person (units) has a 0, whereas the second person (tens) displays a 1. Thus you can see that it takes two people, or two decades, to count to 10. Take a look at any digital clock or watch and note that it takes two counting stages and displays to arrive at 10.

BINARY NUMBERING

No doubt you are aware that a digital computer lacks 10 fingers and appears to operate with only two types of signal: a LED (light-emitting diode) is either lighted or not lighted. This is like having only two fingers. Of course, if you start numbering them, they come out to 0 and 1. There are no more digits because we just ran out of fingers. Obviously the next question is: how can you describe any number, whether positive or negative, with such a severely limited system? Then we ask: how about the letters of the alphabet? Surely some form of magic is at work here.

The answer lies in a number system called "binary" that consists of only two numbers, 0 and 1. These two digits are a natural for a digital circuit, for they can represent either of two states, on or off, the presence or absence of a signal, and so on.

Without going into a basic math course, here is a fast and simple explanation of the binary number system. Use Figure 3.1 as a guide.

Note that the binary code uses powers of base-2, where $2^{\circ}=1, 2^1=2, 2^2=4, 2^3=8$, etc. Note that the result is always twice that of the preceeding result; therefore, $2^4=16$, and so on. Now, if we draw a table like the one shown in Figure 3.1 and, starting from the right, put down the binary code with 2^0 at the right and reaching to 2^3 at the left, we can then put in the decimal values from 1, called the least significant bit, to 8, called the most significant bit.

To create the binary equivalent of some decimal numbers we can start with 0. Because there are no digits in zero, we can start by placing zeros in all four boxes across the line and mark it 0. Because $2^0 = 1$, we put a 1 in the 1s column and 0s in the remainder of the boxes. Thus a 1 can be represented by 0001. Because $2^1 = 2$, we put a 1 in the 2s box and fill the remainder with zeros. Therefore the binary representation of 2 is 0010. We can continue in this way until we have $8 = 1000$.

Decimal	BCD	Octal	Hexidecimal
0	0000	0	0
1	0001	1	1
2	0010	2	2
3	0011	3	3
4	0100	4	4
5	0101	5	5
6	0110	6	6
7	0111	7	7
8	1000	10	8
9	1001	11	9
10	1010	12	A
11	1011	13	B
12	1100	14	C
13	1101	15	D
14	1110	16	E
15	1111	17	F
16	10000	20	10

Figure 3.1 Decimal numbers and their equivalents in BCD (binary coded decimal), octal, and hexidecimal numbering systems.

Now, what about the digits between these numbers? The examples given at the bottom of Figure 3.1 explain how to create these "in-between" numbers. This example reaches only to decimal 15 (8 + 4 + 2 + 1), and a little thought will show you that if you keep extending this pattern you can produce the binary equivalent of any number you can think of; for example, $2^4 = 16$, and if you add this column to Figure 3.1 you can reach 11111 or decimal 31.

Each of the 1s and 0s is called a bit. Now, how many bits does a hobby computer use? Most of the present-day systems use an 8-bit system. Eight bits produce 255 different combinations.

Several of the most popular hobby computers have a series of front-panel switches, and in the Altair, for example, they are arranged as 8 data switches (see Figure 3.2) and 15 address switches. These switches have only two positions, up or down (on or off). There is that binary number system again! The

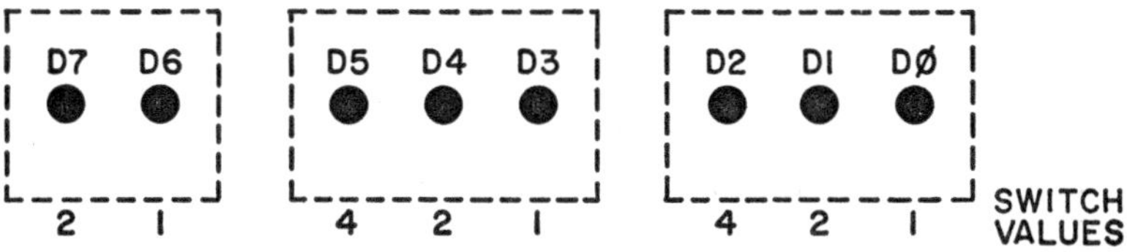

Figure 3.2 Binary data switches arranged in octal configuration (Altair and IMSAI computers).

array of switches, whether data or address, can be set for any number within their limits.

OCTAL NUMBERING

Because the front-panel switches allow only one series of 1s and 0s to be entered, data and address entries may become a dazzling array of easily forgotten combinations of the binary data. Therefore someone had to come up with a new approach that would allow the computerer to remember the wild combinations easily. If you take a look at the Altair, and some other similar computers, you will note that the front-panel data and address switches are arranged in groups of three, starting from the right. This is called "octal," base-8. The usual arrangement is three switches, a small space, three more switches, a small space, and across-the-data and address switches. According to the binary code, each of the three switches has the value of 4-2-1; the 4 is called the most significant bit and is formed by the leftmost switch of the three placed in the ON position. The total of the three switches then forms 7. If we take the lengthy binary number, let us use "11001011" as an example, we can convert this mouthful of digits to something easily remembered. Start at the right-hand side and divide the lengthy binary number into groups of three; thus the example comes out to 11 001 011. Now, using the 4-2-1 approach, by adding up the numbers in each trio we arrive at 313— far easier to remember than the unwieldy 11001011 we started with. Many computer manufacturers use programs that are written in octal, so it will pay you to review these statements.

In many cases the octal number system is easily noticed because no single number among the three is larger than 7. Sometimes after an octal number you will find the subscript 8, which means base-8 or octal.

HEXIDECIMAL NUMBERING

Because eight data switches are found in those computers that employ the front-panel switching scheme, we divide the eight into two groups of four. The switch layout will then be 8-4-2-1, adding up to 15, and we call it hexidecimal or "hex" for short. The word simply means using the base-16 number system.

Now, if you take another look at those front-panel switches (on, for example, the IMSAI), note that they can also be divided into two groups of four by the 8-4-2-1 approach shown in Figure 3.3. Unfortunately, if you start adding up the switch values from zero, all switches down, what happens when you come to 9? What will the next number be? You cannot use 10 because it is a combination of 1 and 0. Why not use letters of the alphabet? This is precisely what is done: A equals 10, B equals 11, C equals 12, D equals 13, E equals 14, and F equals 15.

Now let us return to the binary number we used in the octal description, 11001011. If you set these up on the switches and count the value of each set of four, using the 8-4-2-1 scheme and remembering that 8 is at the left, 4,2 progress to the right, and 1

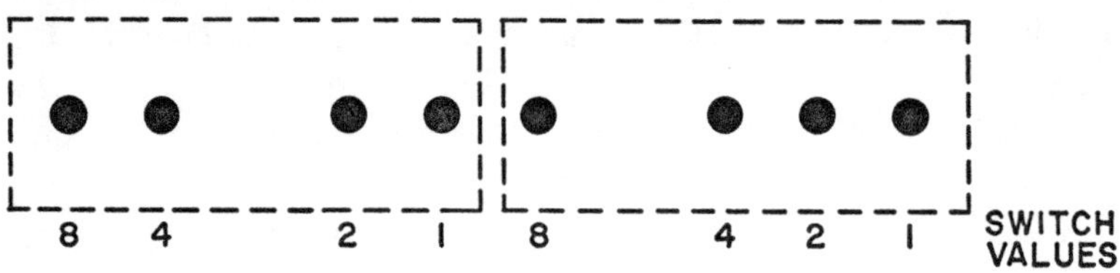

Figure 3.3 Binary data switches arranged in hexidecimal configuration (Altair and IMSAI computers). IMSAI switches are color coded for hex.

is the right-most switch, you come up with the hex equivalent CB, far easier to remember than the awkward 11001011 or even the smaller octal version 313.

So some of the mystery has been removed from octal and hexidecimal notation. In the case of hex the subscript 16 is often used after a hex entry to inform the reader that it is a base-16 number. Most of the time hex can be identified by the capital letters A,B,C,D,E, or F, which may form one or both portions of the 8-bit word.

While we are here it should also be pointed out that the 8-bit word is sometimes called a "byte." Some people call a 4-bit word a "nyble."

There are many other number systems, but because most hobby computers use 8-bit entries we stop our number-system discussion here.

4 The Basic Computer System

Five elements, combined, make up a computer system:

1. The central processing unit (CPU), which in the case of a home computer using a chip is commonly called the "microprocessing unit" (MPU) or "microprocessor."
2. The memory, which stores computer programs and the results of calculations.
3. The input/output (I/O) ports through which data enter and leave the computer.
4. The clock, which causes things to happen in sequence.
5. The power supply, which provides the direct current to the computer.

In addition, there has to be some organization of the various wires or other current-carrying leads that connect the parts of the computer. The arrangement of these leads is called a bus.

Information about the microprocessor and bus structure appears later in this chapter; memory is covered in Chapter 5.

CLOCK

Because a computer system is a complex arrangement of digital hardware, marching to the tune of the software, something has to establish the correct "beat" so that hardware and software can "do their thing" in step. Without correct timing all would be chaos.

The beat in a computer is generated by an electronic circuit called a clock, which emits an accurately controlled electric pulse at certain prescribed intervals. Clock timing is usually controlled by a quartz crystal (like a digital wristwatch) which has excellent stability and will sustain the correct beat for extremely long periods.

The clock signal is then passed to all devices on the bus (except the power supply) and everyone has the same time reference.

I/O

The interface between a computer and the outside world is called a port. Because most ports you will see in hobby computers are both input and output, they are called I/O ports.

The input (I) portion accepts the data from the external device — for example, a keyboard or tape reader — and then prepares them for use by the computer. The output (O) portion accepts the processed data from the computer and prepares them for use by whatever device is electrically connected — perhaps a TTY or CRT terminal.

There are two types of I/O port, serial and parallel. A serial port accepts data from the external device in serial fashion (one bit at a time, sort of digital Indian file) and returns the processed data to the associated output device in the same way. Special circuits in the port have already been set up to determine the speed (called baud rate) of the serial transmissions.

Parallel ports accept and deliver all the multibit data words at one time; therefore these ports operate much faster than serial ports. Some computers use a combination in one device; for example, a keyboard will input data in parallel fashion and a port will output data in serial fashion for use by a serial device such as a TTY or CRT terminal.

THE MICROPROCESSOR

A basic microprocessor consists of a number of specialized logic circuits, all arranged on a single semiconductor "chip" called a microprocessor — sometimes called an MPU (microprocessing unit) or CPU (central processing unit). Figure 4.1 is a simple block diagram.

The thick arrows that interconnect certain blocks mean that several lines join these items.

This device contains a number of registers (storage areas) and a master control system. The ALU (arithmetic logic unit) performs digital addition and subtraction of two input "words" and can detect such things as equality between them.

Two numbers are added by placing them in separate registers, then adding (or subtracting) them and placing the result in another register. If there is any "overflow" from the arithmetic operation, a "carry," called a flag, is generated.

Figure 4.2 describes the basic approach. Here, we are going to add 1 + 2. We are using a 4-bit "word" in this illustration. In the first column (1) we have a 1 and a 0. If they are added, the result is a 1, which is placed in the third register (bottom). The next column (2) contains another 0 and 1 whose total is also 1 and is placed in its box in the bottom register. The other

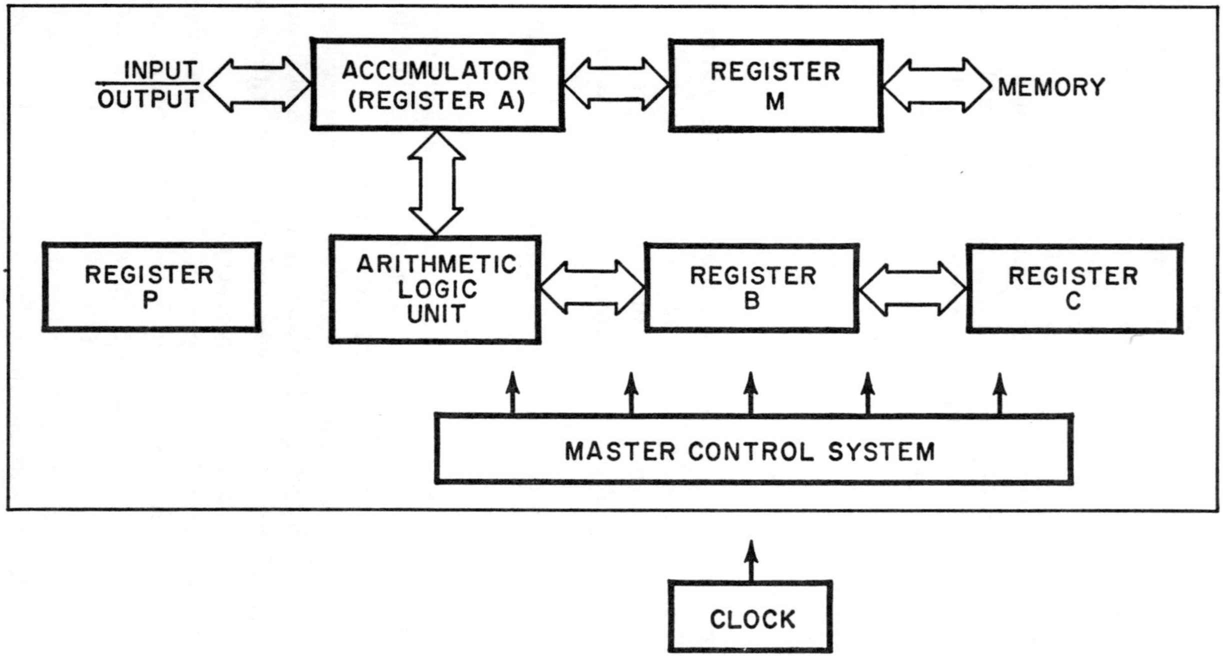

Figure 4.1 Simplified block diagram of a microprocessor. A double-ended arrow indicates that the signal passes in both directions. A broad arrow indicates multiple lines. The clock synchronizes the operation of the system.

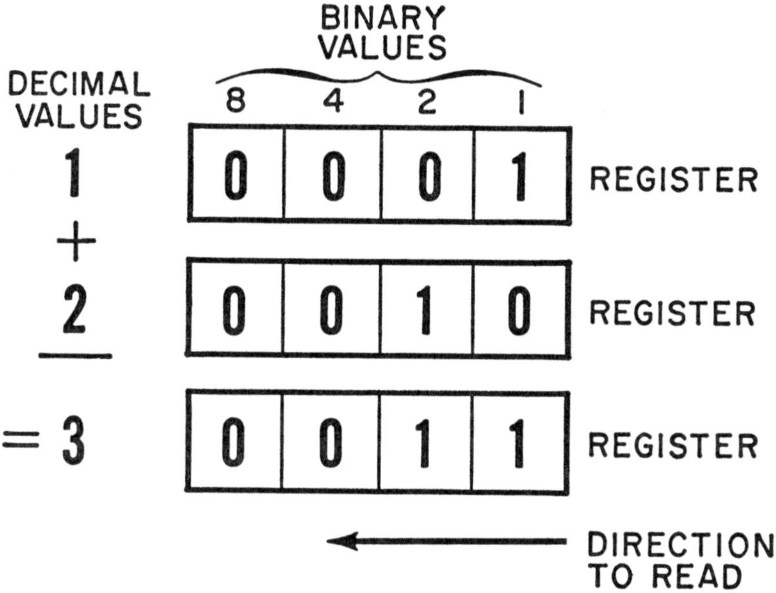

Figure 4.2 Simple binary addition.

two columns (4,8) contain 0s; their total is 0. The result, shown in the lowest storage register, is 0011, the binary equivalent of 3. (Count up the values in the 1,2,4, and 8 columns.)

To illustrate a "carry" Figure 4.3 shows the addition of 1 + 3. In the 1 column we have two 1s, and because they add up to a sum greater than can be expressed in a single binary bit (remember that binary has only two digits — 0 and 1) the total becomes 0 with a 1 to "carry" over. This makes the next column (2) a 1, plus the 1 from the carry. Again this total is greater than a binary 1 and we make this column a 0 with a 1 carry over. The third column (4) contains two 0s; therefore a 0 plus a 1 equals a 1. The total of 0001 plus 0011 equals 0100 — 4 in the binary code.

A processor can contain many registers, referred to as data, working, or scratch-pad memories, which it uses for temporary

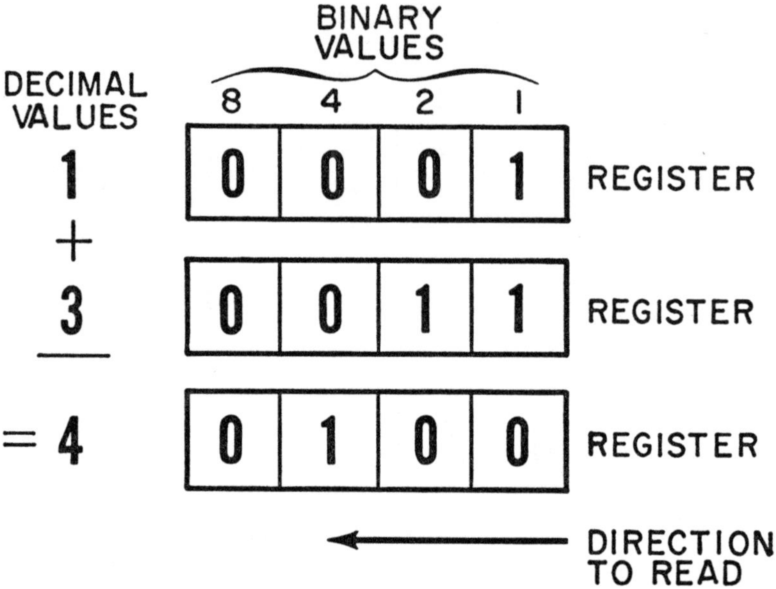

Figure 4.3 Binary addition illustrating carry.

data storage (usually for intermediate results) during data manipulation. Another register (register-P) is used as the program counter which keeps track of each step that the processor will follow in the prescribed series of operations.

The accumulator register is one of the most important sections in the processor because, as you can see in Figure 4.1, all incoming and outgoing data must pass through it. The accumulator can also do other things to the data too complex to cover in this introductory book.

The control unit is a group of elements that provides "instructions" to the remainder of the logic circuits to maintain proper control. The control unit gets its orders from the computer instructions inserted by the user. You can visualize the control unit as a traffic cop handling traffic at a busy intersection. This operations center of the processor sets up the sequences in machine

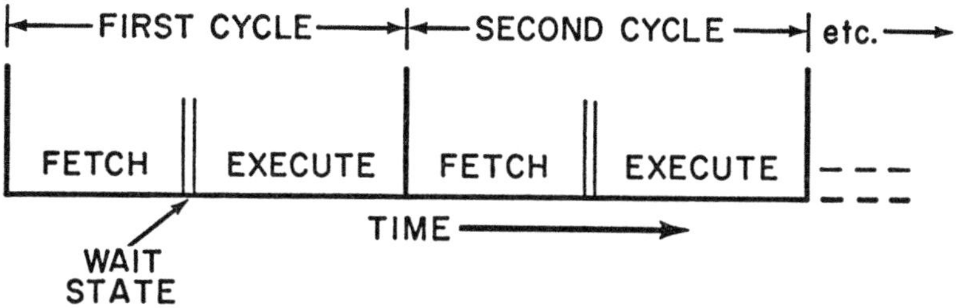

Figure 4.4 The fetch/execute cycle.

cycles (pulses); that is, the entire program is controlled by an electronic clock and all elements do their thing to its "beat". In this way order is maintained.

The processor's two basic operations are called fetch and execute. In the fetch operation data stored in some part of the memory are "fetched" and placed in a register. The next step—execute—then performs the operation selected by the pertinent instruction. In Figure 4.4 you can see how the processor fetches and executes in step with the machine clock (cycles). Sometimes the fetch cycle is extended slightly by what is called a wait state to allow the memory enough time to locate the requested data. Keep in mind that some memory chips are slower than others. The wait state allows slower memories to work properly within the system. The speed of memory operation is called access time and is usually specified in nanoseconds.

Not all processor instructions are 8-bits (eight bits equal one byte) and some are two or three bytes long; for example, you cannot tell a computer to "input" something unless you specify where that something is and what to do with it. The 8080 instruction to input is DB (in hex). However, you must also tell the computer what to input and where it is; therefore more instructions are needed. An example of this is DB 01, which means (in 8080 language) accept an input from input port 1. By the same token you cannot tell the processor to output something unless you specify what you want outputted and where. If you want the computer to "jump" to a particular memory location, you must tell it to jump (C3 in 8080 lingo) and then insert the address; C3 00 10, for example, means jump to memory address 1000 (hex). Note that the jumped-to address is backward, with the least significant digits (00) placed first and the most significant digits (10), last. This "backward"approach is a feature of several processors.

THE BUS STRUCTURE

A bus is a group of leads that carries all the electrical signals to and from the processor. The leads may be wires, copper traces, or a printed circuit board. The Altair, IMSAI, Sol, and some other computers use the S-100, which because it was built by MITS, the developer of the original Altair, is commonly called the Altair bus.

The S-100 is formed by a 100-line set of copper foil traces on a large printed circuit (PC) board, sometimes called a mother board. These lines (not all of which are in use at once, some being available for future expansion) are electrically connected to the CPU board, clock, and power supply. The user can then "plug" 20 or so devices such as memories and I/O ports into the bus merely by inserting the selected device into one of the 100-pin connectors. The actual signals carried on the Altair and similar bus structures are shown in Figure 4.5 and Appendix B. Keep in mind that the hobby computer demand is growing rapidly and that this bus structure may be modified by the time you have read this description.

The "pin out" of the 8080 is shown in Figure 4.5 and the reader can see how the 8080 mates with the classical computer bus structure in Figure 4.6.

The bidirectional DATA bus carries the D0 through D7 inputs and outputs from the CPU to the outside world or from the outside world to the CPU. Special chips in the circuit allow the

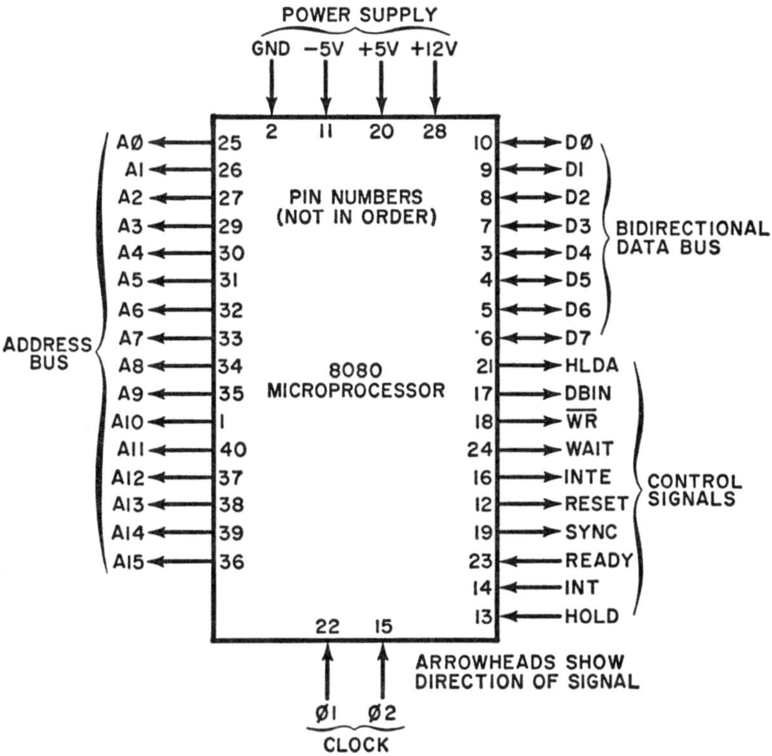

Figure 4.5 8080 pin identification ("pin out"). The 8080 microprocessor has 40 pins, each carrying its own signal in or out of the chip. This chart identifies each pin by number and signal.

data to travel both ways on this bus without interference. This is accomplished essentially by a form of high-speed electronic switching and precise timing (from the clock); the electronic switches are set up to allow the data lines to "output" from the CPU at a certain time before switching over to permit the CPU to receive data.

The ADDRESS bus is only one way — from the CPU to the external circuits. Everything tied to the address bus has its own unique "address," a special bus-coupling circuit wired so that

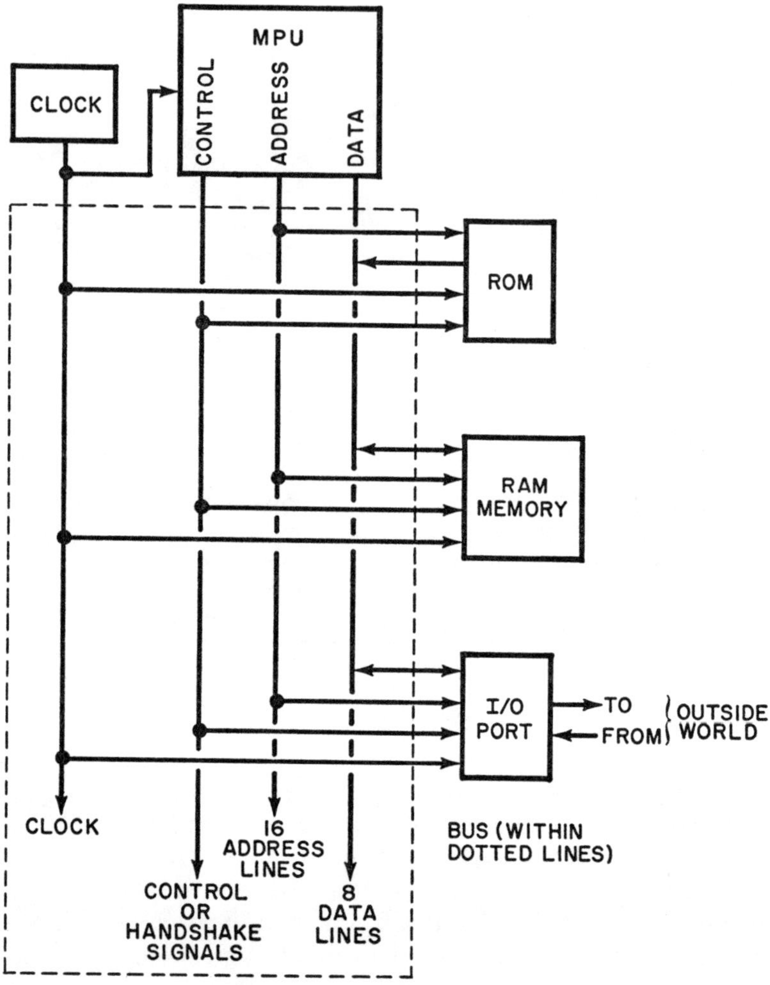

Figure 4.6 A microprocessor system: five basic elements plus the bus structure. The bus structure (everything within the dotted lines) carries all interconnecting address, data, "handshake" control, power, and ground signals.

only that specific address will allow data to pass either way — no other address will work.

This arrangement permits the CPU to select the device or memory with which to "talk" or "listen" and rejects all others. Most hobby computers can handle a couple of hundred external devices.

The CONTROL bus contains the "handshake" signals that tell the non-CPU devices what to do at a particular instant. As shown in Figure 4.6, the control signals include WR (write-read), which tells the memory in which direction the data must flow, RESET to clear everything in preparation for data manipulation, and WAIT to inform the system that for some reason processing has been halted.

The CLOCK line is used to supply the system with the timing signals to give everything on the bus the same time reference; thus all operations will occur in the proper order. The POWER SUPPLY bus provides the required dc power needed by the devices to operate.

Literally dozens of microprocessors are available to the hobbyist. Each type has its own adherents who swear by it (and sometimes at it) and each "does its own thing."

At the time of this writing, and most likely for the next several years, the two most popular types of processor are 8080 (including the Z80) and the 6800 — both available from a number of semiconductor manufacturers. Each is well supported by peripheral "chips" and software.

An in-depth discussion of the "innards" of a microprocessor is beyond the scope of this basic book, but for all intents and purposes they operate in the same way, differing only in "instruction set" and power requirements.

Other computers use buses of different forms, both electronically and mechanically. Therefore you cannot, for example, use Altair-compatible plug-ins with a SWTPC (Southwest Technical Products) 6800 computer and vice versa. Several companies are currently making a wide range of plug-ins for the SWTP-6800 bus structure.

Now you can see that if you are planning to expand your system at some future date it will be best to look for a computer with a supported bus structure in order to take advantage of the many peripherals that can be used with it.

HOW A MICROCOMPUTER WORKS

The microcomputer shown in Figure 4.6 has five basic elements: the MPU which does all the data processing, some RAM memory (RAMs are discussed in Chapter 5), an I/O port (discussed in Chapter 11), and the clock. In the basic system shown an "operating system" (discussed in Chapter 11) is residing in ROM memory (discussed in Chapter 5).

The general operation of the CPU and clock were discussed in the preceding paragraphs and are not covered here.

The bootstrap program in the ROM makes sure that when the computer is first turned on the CPU will automatically "look" at the ROM data for its instructions.

One set of instructions may tell the computer which I/O port to look at first and what to do with the data entering through that port.

In I/O instruction the computer sets up the correct address for that I/O port and then via a set of "handshake" signals turns on that port to make it ready to accept data. The incoming data are then deposited on the data lines. Simultaneously the instructions have told the processor to open the "write" lines to the particular RAM memory. These instructions have also provided the address of that memory, and when this portion of the memory receives the correct address in conjunction with the "handshake" signals the incoming data are deposited in it.

At the conclusion of the data input the processor shuts down the I/O port until is is needed again. The input data are now stored in memory and await use by the operator.

Other instructions stored in the ROM may allow the user to "dump" the stored data into a selected I/O port for rechecking against the original. This dump does not destroy the stored data, for only the "read" line was activated. It allows the data to be displayed only on the selected output device.

To perform the dump the processor simultaneously transmits the address down the address lines, where only the selected device can "pick off" these data, and sends a "read" signal down the control lines. When the two signals coincide, only that particular memory will dump its data onto the data bus. At the same time another address is sent down the line with the appropriate control signals to "open up" the selected I/O port and arrange it so that it outputs data instead of receiving them. The data are now sent to the output device (printer or CRT terminal).

Operating systems also include many other "commands." discussed in Chapter 10.

Thus you can see that under the control of the operating system any element in the computer can be "called" and made to perform its function. The clock makes sure that everything is done "in step" for a smoothly flowing system operation.

In essence, what we are saying is that all elements in the computer that are tied to the address and data lines can be "turned on" by the processor and data can be manipulated between any two elements (or more in some cases) connected to the common bus system. All the processor has to do (under instruction) is send the control signals to the selected device and the data will flow in either direction.

SYSTEM MODULES

Audio Cassette Data Storage

An ordinary Phillips-type tape cassette is used with a conventional audio cassette recorder to store data for future use in the computer. To store data it is converted into audio tones which are then recorded in the tape cassette. There is no standard system of recording the data, however, and data recorded by one system cannot be used by another. The methods with the greatest amount of software support are the following:

1. "Kansas City" or Byte/Lancaster. This system is used by other available interfaces (an interface is an electronic circuit that enables the computer to communicate with external devices) and is accurate but somewhat slow.
2. Tarbell. A popular fast interface that uses a "biphase" method or recording. It loads data fast, has lots of software support, and requires selection of tape recorder units.
3. "ACR" Altair. A method used by MITS on the Altair. Not used by other manufacturers. It is supported only by MITS.
4. Morrow. A popular cassette interface that has a program ROM to simplify its use.
5. CUTS (Computer Users Tape System). A new system developed by Processor Technology for use in the Sol. It has reliable medium speed and good software support and is available for all Altair (S-100) bus machines in a program called CUTER.
6. The Digital Group. A system (or several systems) developed by Dr. Suding of The Digital Group. Available for both Digital Group and other computer systems.
7. Other. The above are only a few of the audio-recording mass storage systems in use. The point in selecting a method is to settle on one that is reliable and has good software support. Once you have made your selection, dedicate at least one cassette recorder unit to your computer for this task.

Video Interface Boards

Video interface boards (e.g., the VDM-1) are essentially CRT (cathode ray tube) terminals without the CRT and sweep systems. These boards plug directly into the Altair bus and deliver monochrome (black and white) alphanumeric characters as "video," which can be applied to a conventional CRT monitor or, via an FCC-approved RF modulator, directly to the antenna inputs of a conventional black and white TV receiver. The VDM-1 is controlled by the computer and forms the O of the I/O port; a keyboard or TTY can be used for the I. This is a low-cost way of producing alphanumerics. If color is your thing, then the Dazzler Video Interface Board, which also plugs directly into the Altair bus, can produce a number of dazzling chromatic displays by using a conventional color TV receiver as the video monitor. All video interface board instruction manuals explain how to connect to a TV set or monitor.

Some of the video interface boards also have a parallel I/O port to permit direct connection of a keyboard. The Polymorphic Video Interface is one, which is a video I/O system may be the only I/O board required. The Digital Group includes the cassette and video interfaces on one board. The MERLIN is a complete video system that produces both alphanumeric output and video graphics. In addition, Merlin has its own ROMs to which a system software monitor may be added.

I/O Boards

Three types of I/O interface board are currently available: parallel, serial, and analog. Many boards are multipurpose; that is, they have a combination of serial and parallel ports on one board (e.g., the 3P+S by Processor Tech and the MIO by IMSAI).

Parallel boards allow for high-speed data transfer; this approach accesses all the data lines at one time and can dump data at high speeds. Serial boards, on the other hand, convert the computer data lines into one serial line and the speed of "talking" can range from a relatively slow 110 baud (bits per second) for the TTY to 9600 baud for some CRT terminals and tape readers. Some form of "on-board" wiring connections allows the user to select the baud rate. Serial interface boards usually provide the 20-mA current loop for the TTY or the RS-232 signal for the CRT terminal.

Analog interface usually means analog-to-digital conversion. These systems change analog (slow-moving) signals such as potentiometers and thermometers into digital words that the computer can understand. Several computer games use joystick potentiometers to move objects around a CRT screen. These joysticks are coupled to the computer by an analog interface. In the not-too-distant future vocal interfaces will be available that will accept analog vocal commands and convert each spoken word into a digital word that the computer can work with.

Digital-to-analog interfaces convert program output into analog signals to provide servo control and relay closures that can be used to turn electric power devices on and off under program control.

Prototyping Boards

A great number of boards with "universal" foil patterns are available to the experimenter. These boards have both wire-wrap and solder-tail IC sockets which permit the design and contruction of circuits that plug directly into a computer bus.

Extender Boards

To troubleshoot a board in an operating computer without causing a short the circuits must be connected to the meter or scope probe. Extender boards plug into the bus and raise the board under test above the level of all others. One altair bus extender, made by Blastmasters (also called Mullen), has a logic probe right on the extender board.

Floppy Disks

As the personal computer develops into the "small business" computer, a better method of mass data storage becomes necessary. The floppy disk fills the requirement for a large-volume, fast-access, easy-to-use system. It comes in "standard" and "minifloppy" versions and is now on the market at prices the hobbyist can afford. Minifloppy disks that use double-density recording and even quad-density recording are on the market as well. This technique extends the data storage capacity of the small disks beyond the capacity of the larger versions.

Other Boards

Solid-state TV-like cameras have also made their appearance. The Cyclops by Cromemco can be interfaced with a digital computer and used for character recognition or in a security monitoring system. More than likely some enterprising experimenters will come up with a TV camera/computer interface that will allow the hobbyist to reproduce all the video effects (in color) that are now monopolized by the TV networks.

It is even possible to "update" your computer to one of the newer high-speed and more powerful CPUs (e.g., the Z80). Several manufacturers are now selling a Z80 board that plugs directly into the bus. In the near future multiprocessor boards will permit selection of almost any microprocessor. OSI, for example, is now offering a board of this kind.

Speaking of updating your computer, until now all hobby computers have used 8-bit processors (and will for some years to come). This means eight data lines. In a few years 16-bit processors will be with us and we shall then have greater (or more accurate) calculating power. Obviously this means that the present bus structure will no longer be used, for it has room for only eight data lines. Some modification of the bus leads will have to be made or a completely new bus structure, designed. However, a set of MPU boards which converts the Altair computer bus into a 16-bit machine is made by Alpha Micro Systems Inc. These boards plug directly into the bus and with their software support make the hobby computer into a machine to rival the minis.

PERSONAL COMPUTING NOW AND IN THE FUTURE

The original hobby computer, like many commercial units, looked like a computer because it consisted of a front panel loaded with switches and LED readouts. Examples include the Altair 8800 and the IMSAI 8080. They are still good systems and can still be found in local computer stores.

These computers used their front-panel switches to insert the "bootstrap" (a machine-language set of instructions that told the computer which I/O port to look at and what to do with the data coming from that port). This also meant that in addition to the basic computer you needed a plug-in I/O port to suit the terminal. Many other functions could be inserted into the computer by using the front-panel switches with the selected address and the data at that address readily observable on the front-panel LEDs. A considerable number of computer hobbyists still feel that front-panel switches are "the only way to go."

Another development is the computer that has no front panel loaded with switches and LEDs. The SWTPC 6800 is a typical example.

In this approach all the necessary computer instructions are contained in a manufacturer's preprogrammed ROM (see discussion of ROM in Chapter 5). All you need to do is turn the computer power on and a prompter symbol appears on the readout. This prompter can be almost any nonalphanumeric character such as a colon or period. Once the prompter turns up, you type in whatever alphabetical characters the ROM needs for it to go into its monitor routine, such as modifying memory, tape input/output, execution of program, or register examination. Each of these ROM systems has its own built-in program, and all information is supplied with the computer. Thus you can see that a ROM system can be handy if your forte is not switch flipping. Besides, the programs built into the ROM are accurate, and there is no way that the user can blow the instructions or put in the wrong one, as when handling front-panel switches.

Because the ROM approach is so convenient, many peripheral manufacturers are presently selling ROM PC boards, complete ROM operating systems built up on Altair-type boards so that hobbyists who have Altair or similare computers can go the ROM route.

The Altair-680b takes advantage of both worlds by incorporating front-panel switches with a ROM system.

Recently a new form of computer came on the market. A number of years ago Sphere pioneered the idea of putting an entire computer system into one package. Processor Technology then developed the Sol (named after one of the authors of this book). The Sol has a keyboard, memory slots, video interface, power supply, cassette interface, and a monitor ROM system in one unit. All that needs to be added is a CRT monitor or an FCC-approved RF modulator if you want to use a conventional TV receiver as the video monitor. The Sol package, looking more like an oversized typewriter than a computer, is aesthetically pleasing and would look well in any home or office. Other manufacturers will most likely follow this example. The old image of lights and a box of switches is on the way out.

5 Thanks for the Memory

Although the microprocessor does all the "thinking," somewhere in the computer there has to be a place to store the required instructions and the results of any data that have been generated. This is called "memory."

Basically there are two types of memory that the hobbyist will encounter—the RAM and the ROM. These are tackled one at a time.

RAM

The word RAM is derived from random access memory, so called because the computer can gain immediate access to any part of it as soon as it determines the required location. The computer does not have to sort through a large amount of stored material and should be able to go directly to where it is needed.

This type of memory is also called volatile because it can "remember" the data stored in it only as long as power is ap-

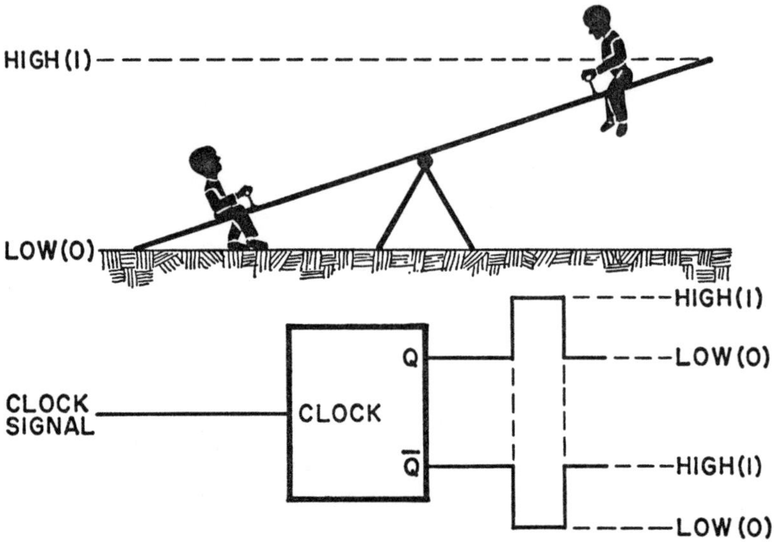

Figure 5.1 How a flip-flop operates. Like a seesaw, a flip-flop has only two stable states.

plied. Once the power has been removed, the memory promptly "forgets," and the next time power is applied it must be "taught" all over again.

Static RAM

Two types of RAM—static and dynamic—work essentially in the same manner. A static RAM means that once a memory cell has been set up to produce a certain output it will remain static in that state until another input pulse causes it to change.

The basic memory cell is called a flip-flop, an electric circuit with two outputs arranged so that when one is high the other is low. These two states can be interchanged, or flip-flopped, an action that can be likened to a seesaw (Figure 5.1). As you can guess, both flip-flop outputs, like both sides of the seesaw, cannot be in the same state at the same time.

The seesaw requires cooperation between two users to change states; that is, the user that was high goes low and the user that was low goes high. This action is known as "clocking."

In Figure 5.1 an electric signal called a "clock" causes the electronic flip-flop to change states. Note that the two output states are arbitrarily called Q and $\bar{Q}$. The bar over the $\bar{Q}$ is called a vinculum which means that $\bar{Q}$ is the electrical opposite of Q. Therefore, when Q is high, $\bar{Q}$ is low. Incidentally, $\bar{Q}$ is described as "not-Q." In most electronic circuits the high state is usually referred to as 1, the low state as 0.

One other thing. If each clock pulse causes the output of the flip-flop to change states, it should (and does) require *two* clock pulses to make each output return to its original state. If you stop to think about this statement, you will see that a flip-flop "divides by two." If you string enough flip-flops together, with the output of one driving the clock input of the next, and so on, it becomes possible to divide the original input clock frequency by almost any amount. This approach is used in many "counting" circuits.

In electronic actuality there is a complex arrangement of transistors in each flip-flop, usually powered by a 5-volt supply. The high (1) output is at almost 5 volts, whereas the low (0) output is at almost zero (or ground). The reason we say almost for both states is that certain electrical properties of the semiconductors that make up the flip-flop do not allow them to reach the full applied voltage or the ground (with the exception of CMOS devices).

Dynamic RAM

The other type of RAM—the dynamic—operates in the same seesaw fashion as the static RAM but with a slight difference.

Revisualize the seesaw and imagine that a "dashpot" (a piston that fits snugly into a cylinder) is attached at the bottom of each side of the seesaw and the ground. Now, when one side is up (high), the action of the two dashpots maintains the position of the two sides, even if the two users want to change states.

Like many other things, the two dashpots leak slightly and are not perfect. This means that after a while they will become ineffective and the two sides of the seesaw can change states.

Now suppose that there is a hose attached to each dashpot and every once in a while compressed air is pumped into each pot. This means that the seesaw can never change states as long as the compressed air overcomes the leak rate.

If, at some time, the users decide to change states, the two dashpots will have to be emptied to allow the change to occur. Once this has happened, the dashpots are "refreshed" with compressed air and the seesaw is again stable in the new state.

In a "dynamic" RAM, the electrical equivalent of this mechanical system, the seesaw is also a flip-flop, and the dashpots are actually some small-valued capacitors in each of its sides. When they carry an electric charge, they maintain the status quo. The "refresh" is performed by the computer. Therefore, when one output is high (1), the other output is automatically low (0). This state of affairs is maintained as long as the charge on the tiny capacitors is "refreshed."

Because the compressed air used by the mechanical dashpots is derived from a pump system somewhere, the charging power for the dynamic RAM's capacitors must also come from somewhere, in which case the associated computer supplies the refreshing power. This, of course, means that computer time must be taken to maintain the refresh cycles. It makes systems using dynamic memory a trifle slower than those using static memory because the microprocessor must take time out from its busy calculating sessions to dash around and refresh the memories. Some dynamic memory plug-in boards have built-in refresh systems which relieve the associated computer from the time-wasting performance of these "housekeeping" chores.

Each flip-flop in a RAM is called a bit, and because most hobby computers use an 8-bit data memory system a number of

RAMs must be used to form a block of memory. Some RAMs, for example, come as 1024 × 1, which means that you will need eight to form a 1K (1024-bit) × 8 memory block, 16 to form a 2K block, and so on. Thus a number of RAMs can be organized as a block of memory, all mounted on a single printed circuit board.

MEMORY READ/WRITE

Now, because a computer may have a number of memory boards, how does it know which block to communicate with? This is done by assigning a unique address to each memory board in the same way that each reader has a unique home address. Mail sent to that address must first find the correct city, then the correct street, then the correct house on that street. Each memory board has a similar problem, which it solves with a special "address trap."

Once the correct address and specified memory (or other) board have been found, special electric signals, called handshake signals, tell the board what the computer wants done with the memory (or other system) occupying that particular location.

Three-State Logic

One other thing about the RAM and some other semiconductor ICs used in computers is called loading.

Visualize a simple ac outlet in your kitchen or workshop. You know that if you keep plugging appliances into that outlet it will eventually blow the fuse. If, however, you turn on only one appliance at a time, the line will not become overloaded and the circuit (fuse) will not blow.

Similarly, if you keep adding devices to a computer signal line, sooner or later the overloading will cause that line to fail catastrophically, and there goes the computer.

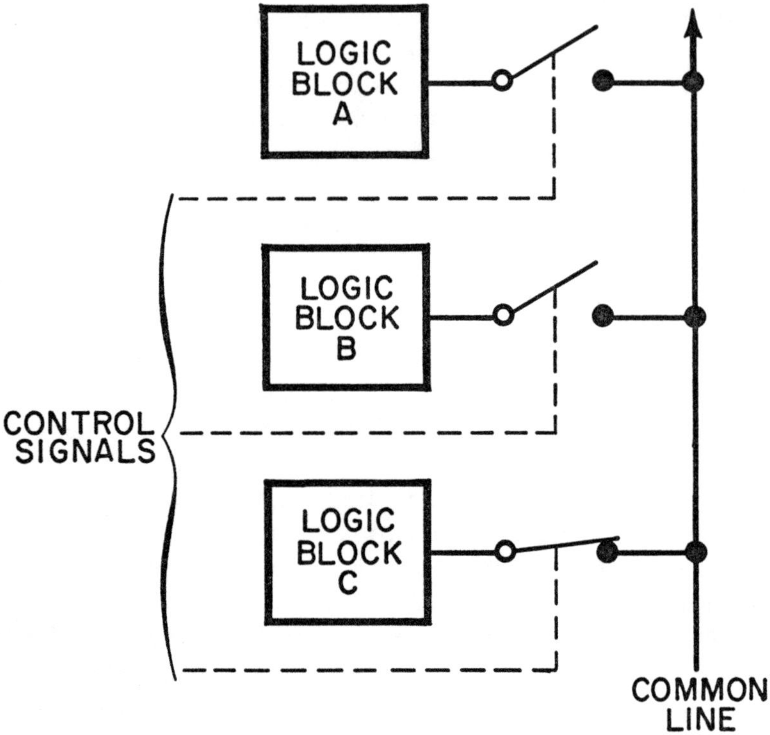

Figure 5.2 How three-state logic works. When the electronic switch is open, the computer never "sees" the associated logic block.

To avoid this problem semiconductor designers have developed what is called three-state logic. This means that when a certain pin on the IC is energized an electronic switch in the IC opens the circuit and effectively disconnects the IC from the computer signal line as if it had never existed. As shown in Figure 5.2, special control signals allow logic block C to tie into the common line, whereas the control signals applied to the other logic blocks cause them to disconnect from it. For all intents and purposes logic blocks *A* and *B* do not exist in regard to the common line.

Thus, with proper control signal timing, literally hundreds of logic blocks can share the same communications line without loading it to destruction. The computer selects the desired logic block with which it wishes to communicate and sends it the control signals.

RAMs are also classified according to access time or how fast a particular RAM can be "talked to" and how fast it will "answer back." These times range from a small fraction of a millionth of a second (nanosecond) to a rather slow millionth of a second (microsecond). In most cases the faster the RAM, the more expensive it is. It is always best, however, to buy the fastest RAMs you can afford.

NEW TYPES OF RAM

In the not too distant future new types of RAM will be coming along. They include the CCD (charge-coupled device) which has a far greater density (more memory cells in a given space on the chip) than present RAMs. It is possible that one CCD RAM could hold the entire 64K of memory that an 8-bit processor could handle. There already is a CCD device on the market that is configured in a 16K× 1-bit format, which means that 16 of these RAMs will fill a present-day computer.

Then there are "bubble memories." This fantastic development works on the principle of extremely tiny bubbles of magnetization, whose axes lie perpendicular to the plane of the single crystal sheet that contains them. These magnetic bubbles are created when two magnetic fields are applied perpendicular to the sheet. Because the presence or absence of magnetic bubbles can represent digital information (1 or 0), these devices can readily form mass memory systems.

Bubble memories are also nonvolatile; that is, they do not lose data when the power is removed. They also have low power requirements; for example, a 10-megabit (10 million bits of data) device requires about 10 watts of power. They have an enormous data density that may reach 2.5 million bits per square inch!

More than likely, when they do come along, one bubble memory device will be enough for an 8-bit computer. It also appears that bubble memories will supplant the relatively expensive floppy disks currently used as mass storage systems. What we have to look forward to in a couple of years is a complete system from computer to mass storage of millions of data words without a single moving part.

ROM

A ROM (Read Only Memory) can be thought of as a RAM whose data are not lost even when the power is turned off. Its read/write circuit has been disconnected so that data cannot be written into it—only read from it.

A page of this book can be likened to a ROM because the written data (words) are not destroyed when the book is closed and put away. When you want to read the printed data, you open the book and turn to the correct address (page, in this case).

Consider a digital calculator, watch or clock. A ROM built into it converts the binary data from the basic calculator or watch function and converts them into the correct readout segment "turn on" to illuminate the correct digit on the seven-segment readouts.

The ROM has many uses; for example, you cannot just turn on a computer and start feeding it data—there is no magic here. After the power is turned on the computer must be given detailed instructions; that is, where to get the incoming data (which I/O port to look at). It must then be fed specific information; that is, what to do with the incoming data. This kind of program is called a bootstrap because the program is entered by its own bootstraps.

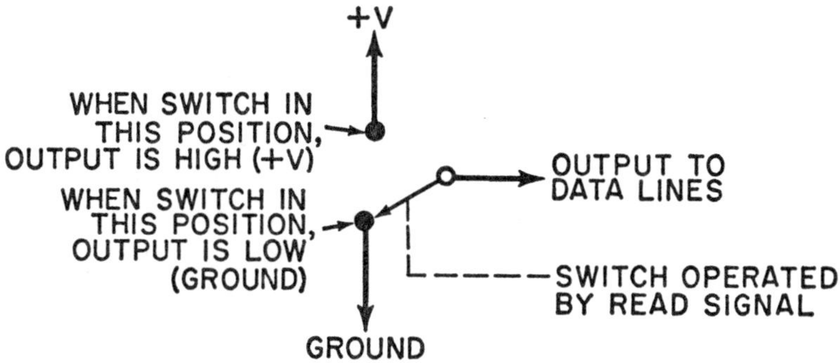

Figure 5.3 A basic ROM.

If you see a computer with no switches on its front panel, the bootstrap is located in a ROM (actually, the bootstrap has been preprogramed into the ROM). If you see a computer with an array of switches and LEDs on its front panel, the chances are that the bootstrap has to be entered by means of these switches, although a ROM has most likely been installed by the owner to save this finger-wrenching problem.

Later on in this book, you will read about "operating systems," "text editors," and "monitors," which are ROM programs devised to make the computerer's life just a little bit easier.

How are data made to stay in the ROM when the power is removed? Well, there are several ways, some of which are briefly described here.

One form of ROM uses a "fusible" link system in which some small, but very real, fuses are "blown" by the application of excessive voltage at certain pins. Once the correct data have been entered in a memory cell, that cell is made to assume the 1 or 0 required; when its associated fuse is blown, the cell remains in that state forever. It cannot be reused to make it form another bit pattern (see Figure 5.3). Typical of these ROMs are the character generators that are blown at the semiconductor factory during manufacture. When the ROM is given a certain bit pattern, it will "output" a bit pattern that is used to form an alphanumeric character.

Consider a digital watch or clock. When the display driver ROM receives a bit pattern, for example, 0111, it will automatically illuminate the correct segments on the display to form a 7.

These ROMs (character generators) can be thought of as Rosetta Stones, which accept data in one language (binary) and deliver them in a form suitable for human use (decimals, in this case, or alphanumerics).

Once an operating system, text editor, or monitor is created, a set of ROMs can be blown to hold the required bit pattern permanently. Many computer hobbyists blow their own ROMs. If you intend to follow this route, take care that your program is correct because once you have blown the fuse that's it . . . no more. Because of the blown fuse links, when power is removed from the ROM the "truth table" (internal bit pattern) is not lost anymore than a house fuse is automatically replaced, as if by magic, when the house power fails.

PROM

Another type of ROM, called the programmable read only memory, which is the backbone of most computer programs, must be permanent in nature. These PROMs, unlike the "blown-fuse" variety, can be erased and reprogrammed by using any of the variety of PROM "burners" available to the computer hobbyist.

PROMs are programmed by the application of a special electric signal and can be erased by the application of another (electrically erasable PROMs) or by the application of a strong ultraviolet light source (UV erasable PROMs) to a special "window" located in the upper surface of the ROM package.

A typical UV cell has its bit pattern determined by the application of a signal that instructs a "floating gate" in the cell to assume a charge that causes the associated cell to produce 1 or 0, depending on the programming signal. This charge is similar to that produced in a dynamic memory cell, but in this case it takes many years to leak off (in some of these ROMs perhaps a 100 years to drop only 30%). These cells may be considered permanent. To erase them a strong UV light source (of a particular frequency) is applied to the window and the floating gates rapidly lose their charge.

Because the UV light requirements are high, conventional room lighting will not erase the PROM. By using a lens you can look through the window and see the chip construction.

Before we leave the area of RAMs and ROMs it must be kept in mind that as a rule they are MOS (metal-oxide-semiconductors) and, as such, must be handled with the greatest care. Always hold them by their case edges and observe all the precautions given in the installation instructions. The static charge that can be built up on your clothes (remember the spark you generate when you walk across a carpeted floor and touch a metal light switch or doorknob?) can reach several thousand volts—at low current. Because most MOS devices are protected to only 100 volts, you can easily "pop" a cell. Of course, once a cell is destroyed, that PROM is finished for all other uses.

HOW MUCH MEMORY DO YOU NEED?

This question has bugged computer hobbyists since the first computer became available to them. The simple answer is: you always need more than what you have!

Parkinson's law states that material always expands to fill the available space (take a look at your attic, garage, or workshop for proof). This law also holds true for the hobby computer. At the start you will usually have a minimum of memory because early learning programs are short and will easily fit the available memory space.

After a minimum of experience you will suddenly discover that the interesting programs your friends have always require more memory than you currently have in your own computer, or one day you will suddenly develop a yen for a high-level language like BASIC (most common among computer hobbyists). Unfortunately, the use of a language in a computer requires memory for its insertion and a little memory space left over to play in.

At the present time you can get 4K, 8K, and 12K BASIC (there is also a Tiny BASIC for use in less than 2K).

This means that you can fit 4K BASIC in a 4K memory with a little left over, 8K in an 8K memory, and 12K in a 12K memory. Be prepared, however, to run out of memory in a short time as your interest and applications grow.

RESIDENT MEMORY

Because most hobby computers use 16 address lines, they can accommodate as many as 64K of memory (actually 65,536 8-bit bytes).

Unfortunately many items, including any ROMs that might support an operating system, monitor, or text editor, "eat" away memory. Other things such as video display modules or other graphic interfaces, floppy disk controllers, and other peripherals also require memory space. All must be deducted from the actual available memory addresses. The documentation (literature such as operating manuals) that comes with these peripherals spells out the memory locations used and how much memory the item requires to run properly.

Once you feel that you have a system you can "live with" you must create a memory and I/O port "map" so that you will always know where each peripheral is located in the memory and how much memory it takes up. The map is created simply by starting with address 0000 at the bottom of the page and working up to address FFFF (hex) at the top. Of course, you can use decimal or octal numbering, but you will find that hex notation is the simplest. The starting and ending addresses of each element that uses memory space should be clearly identified.

By creating a memory map and including I/O port addresses you will always know just what is going on in your computer; whenever you want to "call" something in the memory system, it is a simple matter to look it up in your memory map and go from there.

There may be a mechanical problem, however. If your computer provides for a limited number of "slots" for plug-ins, what do you do?

You can always use large (16 or 8K) memory boards because the more memory you can get into one slot, the more slots left over for other things to plug in (as long as the basic power supply can stand the added load). You will have to arrive at a compromise here, for the larger memories (16K) are far more expensive than, say, 4K memories—each occupies one slot and you will have to look in your wallet to see whether it is worth it. Other ways of having large memories all lie outside the computer.

Mass Storage

Basically, two methods are available, with a third just coming down the pike.

The first two use magnetic storage, either in cassette or "floppy disk" form. Both approaches are discussed in the next section.

Tape

The cassette approach to mass storage employs a conventional low-cost audio cassette in a low-cost conventional audio tape recorder. It is possible to put several hundred thousand bytes on a conventional audio cassette, but the "payment" is in time. Cassette players operate slowly—about several hundred baud per second. Therefore you may have to wait quite a while before you can retrieve your program, especially when Murphy's law states that the one you want now will be located at the far end of the cassette!

Several cassette interface plug-ins not discussed here are covered later on in this book. Each interface, however, has its own address, and if you use any at all be sure to include them on your "memory map."

Disk

This approach to mass storage is new to the computer hobbyist and, at present, somewhat expensive. Many advantages recommend disk storage. The first is that data access time is usually measured in milliseconds (rather than in the minutes of a cassette system). The hobby-sized "minifloppy disk" can hold as many as 100K words, and its actual cost is low (about $4.50 as a rule). Once the initial cost of the disk system and the fact that you usually get a couple of floppy disks (at 100K words each) are taken into account, all subsequent 100K words will cost less than $5. All hobby-sized floppy-disk systems are easily interfaced with a microcomputer, usually by a "disk-operating system" on a PC board that plugs into the computer bus system. Keep in mind that the DOS occupies memory space and must also be included on your memory map.

Incidentally, there are two types of disk system—hard and floppy. The hard disks usually have large memories (1 to 5 megabytes) and come in hard plastic cases. A floppy disk looks more like a piece of dark brown paper in a manila envelope. The disk rotates in the envelope and the record/playback head touches the disk through a small window. Because these disks are soft, they are also "floppy." Floppy disks come in various sizes, ranging from about 5 1/2 to 11 inches in diameter. The larger disks have more memory space.

External Semiconductor Memory

To paraphrase an old saying—a bus is a bus is a bus. To the memory it matters not at all whether they are located in the same enclosure as long as they are all on the same electrical bus.

Several small computer manufacturers are ready to announce external memory systems in which a separate enclosure that carries the same bus as the "mother" computer is inter-connected with the "mother" bus via a multilead connector. Thus, if you have only four slots on your bus structure, you can use one of them to make the connection to the external cabinet that might have the other 15 or 20 usable slots. These external semiconductor memory chassis will probably have their own power supplies to handle whatever load you present to the external bus.

MEGABYTES OF MEMORY

Ever since the first computer was built no one has ever had enough memory to store the next program. The first hobbyists thought they would have if they had 4K memory boards. Then came the cheap, reliable static RAM and 4K boards became obsolete. Every hobbyist then had several 8K boards and were reaching for 16K boards if they could afford them. The semiconductor industry then provided 4 and 16K chips and the race to the megabyte memory was on. One thing was in the way of the big memory bank; the microprocessors in use could address only 65,536 unique memory locations because they had only 16 address lines (2^{16}=65,536). For a while it looked like the memory expansion would have to be done with mass memory devices such as disks, floppies, tapes, and cassettes.

Because computer hobbyists are one of the most inventive groups, a few schemes were soon developed to get around the 64K barrier. First, the memory was organized into external memory banks and installed in a separate cabinet with its own power supply and refresh circuits.

The second method of memory expansion is the IMSAI IMM (intelligent memory management) system, an internal memory expansion scheme in which up to one megabyte of memory can be mounted in an IMSAI computer and addressed by the 8080 microprocessor!

The IMSAI IMM scheme implements memory expansion by providing four extra address lines (16 to 20). The expanded memory is organized into blocks of 16K and as many as 64 blocks can be used (1,024,000 words)! These memory blocks are selected by the added address lines and are switched in and out as required. The switching is done under software control and the entire memory is protected against having its contents overwritten by the system. If an attempt is made to write into protected memory locations, a system interrupt is generated.

The IMM controller and the 32 and 65K memory boards are interesting because they have been developed without any "advanced technology" such as bubble memory or charged-coupled devices. The greatest drawback to the system seems to be the cost. As in other new developments in this field, the high price will decrease and megabyte memories will soon become commonplace. The question most hobbyists and other microsystem users will ask is: "How does this affect me, since I can't afford megabytes of memory?" The answer is that the development of large-capacity memory boards will lead to computers with greater power in a smaller physical space, which, in turn, will reduce cost, without reducing computing power. The smaller machines will also have the capability of expansion by the use of memory-management techniques and memory I/O schemes.

6 What Kind of Equipment Should You Start With?

The most difficult decision in getting involved with your own computer is what to start with. After you have read all the magazines, books, and manufacturers' catalogs you will become even more confused by the conflicting claims and descriptive information. Only one year ago your decision would have been limited to a narrow range of choice. You would have decided on a computer based on the Motorola 6800 or the Intel 8080 microprocessor. Once that choice had been made, you would have decided between the Altair or IMSAI, if you went with the 8080. If you decided on the 6800, you could have picked from the Southwest Technical Products 6800, the Sphere, or the Altair 680. There were a few of the semiconductor manufacturer's one-board evaluation boards around but most of them were unavailable to the general public. Now hundreds of new products reach the market every year, each advertising its merits to people who have discovered the possibility of owning their own computers. One of the main purposes of *this* book is to help potential buyers of computers to make an intelligent choice.

The initial decision, or first equipment purchase, will affect the user's path through the world of personal computing. The parts are costly and most people will be unable to scrap what they buy and start over. Industry can write off an obsolete computer but a hobbyist can only trade or sell old computers that are in demand. The next few chapters offer information to help you to choose. At least they attempt to teach you enough to narrow the choice to units that fit your needs and your goals.

TRAINING DEVICES

Several manufacturers have produced devices that teach microprocessor operation and microprocessor programming. These devices range from complete systems, including professional texts, to simple cardboard simulations. In some cases they are part of a course given by an instructor in a classroom setting. Some of the important points to consider are the cost and time you will have to devote to learning about microprocessors and what use the training device will have when the training is complete. In most cases the training device will have limited use as the foundation of your personal computer; once you have recognized that fact you can decide whether the training you are getting is worth the cost.

The CARDIAC

Several years ago, at Bell Labs, a simple but clever device was developed to teach the basic functions of a computer. Made of cardboard, this gadget is a powerful and practical manually operated computer which comes with a 53-page illustrated manual. A student uses the CARDIAC and the manual to complete a series of 10 different programs which range from simple to complex. The CARDIAC costs under $10 and is an excellent starting place for the neophyte. It is available at computer stores and from the Comspace Corporation in Farmingdale, New York.

Once the beginner has left the field of books and simple teaching aids like the CARDIAC, there is nothing between $10 and more than $100 that will satisfy his urge to own a personal computer.

The Ohio Scientific Model 300 Trainer

The OSI Model 300 Trainer is a completely tested and assembled computer trainer designed to give the user "hands-on" experience in the operation of a microprocessor. The unit comes with a 20-experiment lab manual that starts by loading the contents of the memory. The last experiment describes how to interface a microcomputer to a Teletype. Because the user rarely has a Teletype at this stage, this lesson is mostly theoretical. The Model 300 has no ability to expand into a real computer and has only 128 words of memory (each word being 8-bits). The microprocessor is the MOS Technology 6502. OSI and its dealers charge less than $100 for this trainer and provide an unusual trade-in plan. When purchased under the "Model 315 graduation plan," the user buys the training for a little more than the cost of the trainer. Within 60 days he returns the trainer and gets most of his investment back in OSI 400 system boards and documentation. In this case the user is not left with a device he has outgrown but can progress to a complete computer system at low cost. The original lab manual is kept by the user for reference. The Model 300 is a simple device, and, although the manual is not the easiest thing to learn from, the OSI system does teach microprocessors and the Model 315 plan does provide an open-ended path from the trainer to a working computer.

The Texas Instruments Microprocessor Learning Module System

This learning system represents a major educational effort that integrates a well-written text with a series of learning modules. There are four modules in the system. The basic building block is the LCM-1001, which demonstrates the fundamental level of microprocessor operation, a single-step microinstruction. It has a 4-bit static processor and manual switch inputs. The unit is battery-powered and interfaced to the other modules by a connector and ribbon cable. The first module costs about $150 and really requires the addition of the second and third units at about $190 each to present a more complete picture. The fourth module is I/O at about $110 and teaches the interface between a computer and the external world. In all, the Texas Instruments learning system is an effective way of learning but represents a large expense for the individual, especially when it is considered that the equipment has no other application than as a teaching tool.

Iasis Ia 7301 Computer in a Book

Iasis Inc., which has specialized in microcomputer courses for industry and educational institutions, has developed the Ia 7301 computer-in-a-book concept. This is unusual in that it provides an 8080-based, single-board computer in a looseleaf book which is also a programmed microcomputer course. The course enables the user to learn programming and to operate the computer. One derives actual hands-on experience from the unit. In addition, the microcomputer can be removed from the looseleaf binder at the conclusion of the training and the computer can be expanded to the full 8080-capacity of 64K of memory and 256 I/O ports by the use of optional expander boards. The basic unit contains a hex keypad and LED readout display, 1024 bytes of RAM, 1024 bytes of ROM containing a monitor program, two I/O ports and a cassette tape recorder interface, and three LED indicators that show read and write tape and execute programs. The Ia 7301 is the first training device that leaves the user with knowledge as well as a usable expandable computer.

MICROCOMPUTER TRAINING CLASSES AND SEMINARS

Several of the major distributors of microcomputer equipment hold training classes from time to time. Schweber Distributors have microprocessor centers at several of their locations and classes are often held on the various processors they distribute. There is usally a nominal charge for these intensive classes, which are addressed to people with technical experience. Their purpose is to encourage engineers to design equipment by using microprocessors. If you inquire about the courses, the instructors will describe the cost and technical level required to absorb the information.

Many computer stores give courses from time to time and most of the amateur computer clubs have some kind of instruction. One thing to consider in signing up for any course is the cost of the equipment associated with it. In some cases the fee includes a one-board type of microcomputer which the student keeps after the course. The cost of this trainer may increase the price of the course to a rather high level, and the buyer should carefully consider whether the equipment he is being sold will have any use in his future system. Most of the clubs either do not charge or require only nominal fees for instruction or membership dues. They usually do not tie the student into an equipment purchase.

The personal computer is recognized by colleges and high schools as an educational tool, a subject of interest to the student body, and the public in general. Many schools are now giving courses as part of regular programs and as extracurricular activity. In addition, microprocessors and personal computing have become popular subjects for adult education and schools of general education sponsored by universities and public school districts.

EVALUATION KITS

Almost all the semiconductor manufacturers who make microprocessors offer evaluation kits intended for engineers of industrial companies. The purpose of these kits is to provide a low-cost way of determining just how a microprocessor would work in industrial products. In most cases these kits contain a "bare-bones" operation consisting of the processor, a minimum amount of random access memory (RAM), and the simplest kind of firmware program in a programmed read only memory chip (ROM). This monitor program permits the user to examine the contents of the RAM memory and to change it in a step-by-step procedure. The evaluation kit is designed to operate in conjunction with a Teletype or other terminal, which may be expected to exist in any engineering department. Because this book is about personal computers, it does not attempt to cover all of these evaluation kits. The hobbyist is not advised to try to expand one of these kits into a complete personal computer unless he has considerable experience. They are not made for personal computing applications. However, once the user has acquired a much broader background, he may adapt a kit for special control uses.

This book discusses the one-board computers which are different from the evaluation kits in complexity and application. It may sometimes be difficult to tell the difference between a practical one-board computer and a simple evaluation kit. You must consider the features offered on the board and their potential for expansion into a usable computer system. You must also consider the kind of work you want to do with your machine. If it is any kind of data processing application, a higher level language will be needed. The smallest of these high-level languages, Tiny BASIC, needs 2000 (8-bit) words of memory to contain the language. An additional amount of memory is required for the user's program to be written in BASIC and still more memory to store data. It turns out that about 4000 (4K) words of memory are needed for any small application program in BASIC. Boards or machines that offer less to start require immediate expansion for practical use. The buyer should make sure that memory expansion is possible without too much trouble or great cost. In addition, the user should give thought to the means of getting data into and out of his machine. Teletypes are expensive and blinking lights or LED characters are not satisfactory for long (see Chapter 11).

ONE-BOARD COMPUTERS

This type of computer is the most confusing but also the largest group of machines on the market. Some judgment must be made about its application. Many one-board computers have been designed for use by industrial OEMs (original equipment manufacturers) to be built into other machines to provide intelligence or control. We are already seeing these applications in automobiles, washing machines, and other appliances. Sometimes the one-board computer becomes part of some other computer peripheral such as a terminal used for word processing or a mass data storage system. Often the industrial manufacturer need not reinvent anything but can buy a ready-made, one-board computer for his application. This is the real power of the microcomputer. It is a general-purpose device that can do many tasks with software rather than by specialized electronic circuitry. In the past a manufacturer may have offered different models with various options. Today he can program his options into the internal computer and upgrade merely by changing the program! The designers of the OEM one-board computers have been clever in providing numerous features, and some of the units have direct application for personal computing. At this time new types are coming into the market almost daily and this book may miss some. The buyer should consider the following guidelines in making his choice.

Guidelines for One-Board Computers for Hobbyist Use

1. Has it an operating system on ROM to allow the operator to do the following:

   Go to any memory location, examine the contents, and change them if desired?
   Step to any memory location? Reset?
   Load a tape and punch (or record) a tape?
   Easily run a program?
   Use a standard set of instructions provided by the manufacturer of the microprocessor in hex (or octal)?

2. Does it contain I/O provisions in both serial and parallel form? Is there a choice of RS-232 or 20-mA current loop output for the serial output?
3. Has it a cassette interface or provision for one?
4. Is a practical method provided for memory expansion? By practical, we mean a method of expanding memory that does not require a user to build his own memory-bus structure. There should be room on the board for additional memory boards to plug directly into the main board.
5. Can a power supply for the computer be easily obtained at reasonable cost? Some one-board computers provide power supplies at optional cost, in which case the user should take

the supply offered if he wishes to avoid trouble in using the unit. When estimating the full cost, include the power supply offered; for example, with the Apple computer the manufacturer has included an on-board power supply, less the power transformers. These are ordinary transformers obtainable at most electronics supply stores. If nothing is said about the power supply except a statement of power requirements, investigate the cost and trouble you will have to go through to get the proper supply.

6. Are replacement or expansion ICs available from hobbyist sources? Many one-board computers achieve their compactness by using chips that are new or not readily available to hobbyists. This means that replacements are obtainable only from manufacturers or industrial distributors. Often such distributors and manufacturers are not set up to deal with hobbyists' repair and replacement requests.
7. Is there a high-level language available (i.e., BASIC)? Because many one-board computers are sold as "development systems," the manufacturers do not provide "resident" high-level language support. A high-level language that is resident on a time-sharing system and produces machine code for use on a microcomputer is not much use to the hobbyist. BASIC, or its equivalent, must be capable of being resident in the computer and must be supported by enough RAM to run a usable program. Do not be impressed by the fact that there is a lot of software for the particular microcomputer chip. Often the software for one computer cannot be run on another computer that uses the same microprocessor. An example is the KIM-1 and the Apple-1. Both use the MOS Technology 6502 microprocessor. However, the manufacturer of the Apple computer provides its BASIC on the ACE cassette unit which runs at 15 times the speed of the KIM cassette. There is no direct way of using Apple BASIC with the KIM. On the other hand, there is a version of Tiny BASIC for almost all versions of the 6800 and the 6502 chips.

8. Has the design provided for some physical expansion of the system? The mere existence of a connector with the data, address, control, and power lines is not enough for full expansion of the one-board computer into a system. Some attention must be given to the orderly expansion of the group of boards by a unified bus. An excellent example of the use of a bus without sacrificing the flexibility of board selection is The Digital Group system for which the user has the choice of processors and still retains the advantages of a mother board and bus structure. OSI also uses a bus structure that permits growth from a single board computer to a complete system without external cables. In fact, OSI systems have expanded other 6502 microcomputers, such as the KIM-1.

MAINFRAME COMPUTERS

Mainframe computers usually feature an enclosed cabinet (generally metal) that houses a suitable power supply sufficient for full computer expansion, an address and data bus arranged so that peripherals can be plugged in, a processor board and its associated logic elements, and (if used) front-panel controls. It is the electromechanical bus system that allows for later system expansion because all the required signals and power lines are available on one plug-in bus.

In most cases the user also has to supply a terminal such as a Teletype or CRT monitor so that the user can "talk" to the computer and the computer can "answer" back.

This, of course, means that the computer must have a suitable I/O (input/output) port to mate the terminal to the computer. Some computers have an I/O port built in, whereas others, such as the Altair or IMSAI, require the user to supply the I/O port, usually on a single plug-in board.

Video modules that generate the entire spectrum of alphanumeric characters can be purchased for most computers (the

Processor Technology VDM-1 for the Altair/IMSAI machines is a good example). These modules are plugged into the computer bus system and under computer control generate the composite video signal required by a CRT monitor or modified TV set. Of course, if you elect to go this route, this takes care of the output port, but you will still need a keyboard and some means of getting the keyboard data into the computer input port. Once again, you can purchase I/O boards made by several peripheral manufacturers or by the computer manufacturers themselves.

What all this means is that the cost of various peripherals required to make the computer "talk" must be added to the initial cost of the computer.

The new generation of hobby computers, such as those represented by the Sol Terminal Computer produced by Processor Technology, come with everything included—CPU, control logic, keyboard, cassette interface, RAM memory, ROM monitor, power supply, I/O ports, and the necessary bus expansion connectors. All you need for this approach is a CRT monitor. Although at the time of this writing Sol is one of a few "all-in-one" computers available, others will no doubt follow this efficient approach.

Probably the largest single area of cost (other than the computer itself) is in the memory system. Therefore, before selecting any computer, check around to make sure that reasonably priced blocks of memory are obtainable from at least two different sources—just in case one source dries up.

KITS VERSUS READY-BUILT COMPUTERS

There are three ways of getting your own computer: buy one already built and tested, get someone to build a kit for you, or build it yourself. The first two are the easiest but in general the most expensive, about 40% more. Also, you will learn very little about how your computer operates and will be at the mercy of others if anything goes wrong and has to be repaired.

The best way is to build your own. Of course, this means that you will have to know how to use a soldering iron, be able to read schematics, know what all the parts look like, and so on. You should also have some kit-building experience before you tackle the job, although building a computer is not that difficult. A little hardware experience and a lot of patience and common sense are all that is required.

If you feel like "having a go at it" but are afraid, then it is suggested that you start with a simple electronic kit; for example, a Heathkit or equivalent multimeter or scope. Besides the kit-building experience, you will end up with an excellent piece of test equipment that can be used later on. Experience has shown that the Heath assembly manuals are easier to understand than many provided with hobby computers which assume some knowledge of hardware.

If you already have (or once you have) acquired some hardware experience, you should be able to follow the detailed assembly instructions that come with most computers. Simply follow the steps and do not skip around. Check and double check each one before performing it (especially on the color code for resistors) and use sockets for all ICs and transistors even though they may be called out as optional. Keep in mind that it is easier to exchange a suspect IC or transistor when it is in a socket than to unsolder it and take a chance of ruining it and the thin copper foil it sits in with excessive heat.

TOOLS

You do not need a great many tools to assemble a computer or any of its peripherals. A 25-to 35-watt soldering iron (not a gun) with a reasonably sharp tip is a must. The tip of the iron must be kept clean by wiping it occasionally on a piece of damp cloth. Only fine, thin rosin-core solder should be used. Stay far away from the acid-core type. Most kit warranties are void if you use acid-core solder.

Several other low-cost tools are among those that a kit builder should have: a pair of sharp diagonal cutters (although toenail clippers will also do a good job), a pair of long-nose pliers for forming leads and holding small components while soldering (a form of protective heat sink), and a pair of conventional gas-pipe pliers for tightening mounting hardware on metal chassis and adjusting controls such as switches and potentiometers.

A variety of small screwdrivers, including large and small Phillips types, will also come in handy. Several spools of color-coded hookup wire, solder lugs, and assorted nuts, bolts, and washers should be provided. Electrical tape and, if possible, several sizes of heat-shrinkable tubing will help to make good connections.

During the last year or so another form of connection making called wire-wrap has come along. This technique does not require soldering but it does call for some special, low-cost tools. Take a look at what your local computer store stocks for this new wiring technique and do not be afraid to try it out. The wire-wrap approach is great when you are building an experimental circuit and need to change the connections. Instead of having to unsolder a device and probably "hack and chop" PC foil patterns wire wrapping allows you to make the circuit change merely by unwrapping the selected wire and routing a new one. Of course, wire-wrap sockets and connectors are essential.

Other tools, not so commonly known, can certainly come in handy: a magnifying glass (two-to-four power is sufficient), a bright workshop lamp (100 watts), a small and sharp awl or other sharp-pointed tool, a toothbrush, and a solder sucker or some lengths of coaxial-cable copper braid (solder wick).

When assembling a PC board, the magnifying glass is used to examine a solder joint and inspect the foil traces for accidental solder "bridges" (in some places the slender copper foil traces lie close together and it is easy for the molten solder to form a "bridge" between adjacent traces and thus create a short). If this does occur you can use the solder sucker or the coaxial cable braid (lay the braid on top of the unwanted solder and heat the combination with a soldering iron so that the solder will flow into the braid) to remove the excess. After all the obvious "blobs" have been cleared up, the board should then be examined under the magnifying glass and bright work light and the sharp awl used to clear away any debris between foil traces or IC lead pads. The loosened debris can be brushed away with the toothbrush.

Actual construction can take place on a kitchen table or workbench as long as there is sufficient illumination. Do not rely on ceiling fixtures or distant lamps for light; they cast too many shadows.

A set of stackable plastic boxes is useful for storing small and easy-to-lose parts; the contents of each should be clearly identified. A conventional 12-to 16-place muffin pan, sold by all hardware stores, makes a handy temporary storage place for the small parts that go onto the board.

Before starting contruction check that all parts are there. Most construction manuals contain parts lists; as you remove each part from the shipping container, check off the pieces on the list provided. They can then be stored in the plastic boxes and fed to the muffin pan for use in a particular series of steps.

Follow the written instructions carefully. After reading each step to make sure that you understand what you have to do pick up the item to be installed, check it against the parts list (particularly for the correct resistor color code or IC identification) and any accompanying illustration, and insert it in place. Sometimes it is best to "tack solder" (very lightly solder one pin in place) and then check the installation from the other side of the board to make sure that you are fitting the component into the correct set of holes before final soldering.

After the installation of all components is complete recheck the finished board against the manual photograph, or component installation, to make sure that the correct resistors are in the correct places, that polarity markings on electrolytic capacitors are on the correct side, and that the ICs have their pin-1s in the correct position. Also check the bases, emitters, and collectors of the transistors for proper placement.

If the board uses MOS-type semiconductors, make sure that you follow the manual instructions for installing this type of IC or transistor; otherwise you will find them catastrophically damaged by static electricty.

Most computers, and computer peripherals, include a number of tests, both voltage and signal, that can be made for correct assembly and operation of the system. These tests generally require the use of a multimeter or oscilloscope or possibly an I/O port. If you do not own any of these items, talk to the members of your computer club or to the people at your local computer store. Most hobbyists and stores will be glad to help. This is one of the major advantages of belonging to a computer club or dealing with a computer outlet.

7 Altair, IMSAI, and Other Machines Using the S-100 Bus

To the best of our knowledge the Altair 8800, which was introduced in the January 1975 issue of *Popular Electronics*, was the first hobby computer made available in kit form.

Because it was the first, and soon the best seller, many of its elements became the *de facto* standard among computer hobbyists. The most famous of these elements is the Altair bus referred to earlier.

Two Altairs use this bus—model 8800A and the newer 8800B.

ALTAIR 8800A

This machine is described here in a little more detail than the others because it formed the basis for the other two.

Model 8800A consists of a metal front panel mounting 15 toggle switches (in octal format) along its length. All 15 switches are used to "address" the memory, whereas the first eight do double duty, for they also act as data input switches.

Another row of eight switches along the bottom of the front panel is used to STOP/RUN the computer, SINGLE-STEP through a program, EXAMINE/EXAMINE-NEXT the memory locations, DEPOSIT/DEPOSIT-NEXT data into the selected address, RESET/CLEAR the entire system so that it will start up at address zero, and PROTECT/UNPROTECT blocks of memory so that data in those blocks will not be "written over" and thus destroy the program painfully inserted by the front-panel switches. Two AUXiliary switches, used to turn on peripheral devices, were also included. The mainpower switch was situated on the far left of the bottom row and spaced far enough away from the other switches to prevent the machine from being accidentally turned off as the user reached for other operating switches.

A row of LEDs (light-emitting diodes that glow red when power is applied) is mounted above each of the 15 address/data switches, and when any LEDs are lighted it indicates that the selected switch (or function) is activated. The eight data switches have their own LEDs arranged above each data switch and above the accompanying address LED.

Other LEDs are used to indicate computer status: whether or not the memory being addressed is protected and whether the computer is stopped or running.

Mechanically, the front-panel switches and LEDs are all part of a single large printed circuit (PC) board that is mounted directly behind the metal front panel; all switches and LEDs protrude through holes in the metal face plate. This board is connected to the bus structure by a multilead cable that connects the data lines to the microprocessor plug-in board. The bus of the Altairs runs parallel to the front panel.

The bus structure in the Model A is formed by a number of expansion boards, each having the 100 lines that form the bus etched in its copper foil. Provision is made on each expansion board for mounting four 100-pin connectors (arranged with 50 connections on a side). Each end of each expansion board has 100 solder pads which permit the boards to be interconnected by a number of jumpers. A pair of mounting rails is mounted on the chassis to which the expansion boards can be affixed, side by side. Thus the first expansion board connects to the multiconductor cable from the front panel and supports the microprocessor board with its 8-lead interconnection to the front panel. Each plug-in board has 100 edge connector "lands"—50 on each side of the double-sided boards—and each can be plugged into the 100-pin bus connector.

Thus in a basic system the first expansion board can support the microprocessor board, an I/O port, and a couple of memory boards. Because allowance is made for only four plug-ins, expansion boards must be added as your plug-in needs grow.

The computer power supply, arranged along the rear wall of the chassis, uses a long slender PC board to support the smaller electronic components. This power can support a full complement of add-ons, and an optional fan can be mounted at the rear of the chassis if long operating times, hence higher temperatures, are expected.

The rear panel also includes cutouts for eight connectors to the outside world; for example, Teletype or CRT monitor. The case is provided with ventilation louvers, and four small rubber feet on the bottom keep cooling air circulating.

ALTAIR 8800B

This newer version of the famous Altair 8800A has the "look" of its famous predecessor but has been greatly upgraded electronically, electrically, and mechanically.

The front panel has taken on a new appearance with the addition of large bat-handle switches and submerged LEDs that can be seen only when they are lighted. A new plastic dress panel protects the front-panel markings from being spoiled by accidental rubbing over. The physical arrangement on the front panel has not been greatly changed.

The old AUX switches have been removed and replaced with a new pair: ACCUMULATOR DISPLAY/LOAD and INPUT/OUTPUT. Now the old SINGLE-STEP switch has two positions, SINGLE-STEP used as before and the new SLOW position.

This new position permits the user to single-step through the program, but instead of doing it manually with the single-step switch he now places the new switch in the SLOW position and the circuit does an automatic single step at two machine cycles per second.

The new ACCUMULATOR positions are more useful to an experienced programmer than to a beginner. Essentially, they permit the display and loading of the 8080 accumulator register.

The old front-panel PC board has been replaced by a display /control board that conditions (debounces, etc.) all the front-panel switches and information to be displayed on the front-panel LEDs. It also contains a PROM that performs the various operations selected by the front-panel switches. This board is connected to the remainder of the system by a pair of board-edge connectors and a multilead cable, the other ends of which terminate in connectors on a new interface board that conditions all the signals between the new front panel and the bus. It also contains the eight parallel data lines that are routed to the CPU board.

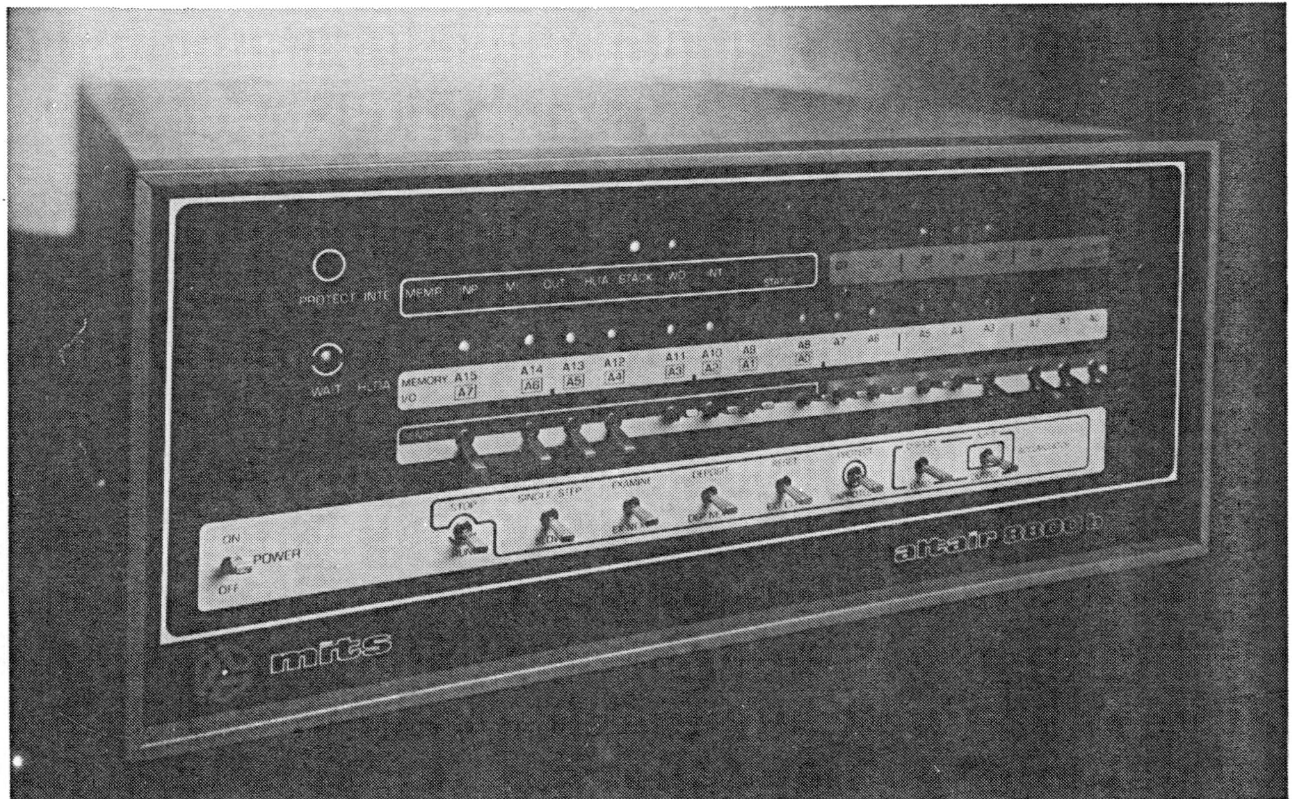

Altair 8800B

Many other electronic, electrical, and mechanical changes have improved the Altair, chief among which is the inclusion of a bus mother board that contains 18 connectors for the optional plug-ins (opposed to only four in the old expansion boards). The power supply has been beefed up to accommodate the future plug-ins.

IMSAI 8080

This machine, which bears a strong resemblance to the Altair, appeared on the market in kit form shortly after the Altair made its debut. It is also an 8080-based system and features the Altair bus.

Mechanically, the IMSAI 8080 is distinguished by its bold front panel whose paddle switches have large handles and are brightly color-coded. Its bus structure is at right angles to the front panel (runs from front to back in the chassis) and is designed with a single mother board that provides for 22 plug-ins. The power supply, which is one of the largest in the industry, can produce up to 28 amperes, more than enough to operate with a full mother board.

The IMSAI front panel plugs directly into the mother board via the 100-pin edge connector. The front panel, like the Altair 8800B, is covered with heavy-duty plastic but also includes eight program-controlled LEDs that can serve a variety of display functions. The front-panel, mother-board, plug-in concept can be configured to allow the IMSAI 8080 to operate as a "turnkey" system without a front panel.

SOL

As mentioned earlier, Sol represents a new look—a full computer without its appearance. There is nothing that new in Sol. It is a basic computer that takes all the elements that had to be

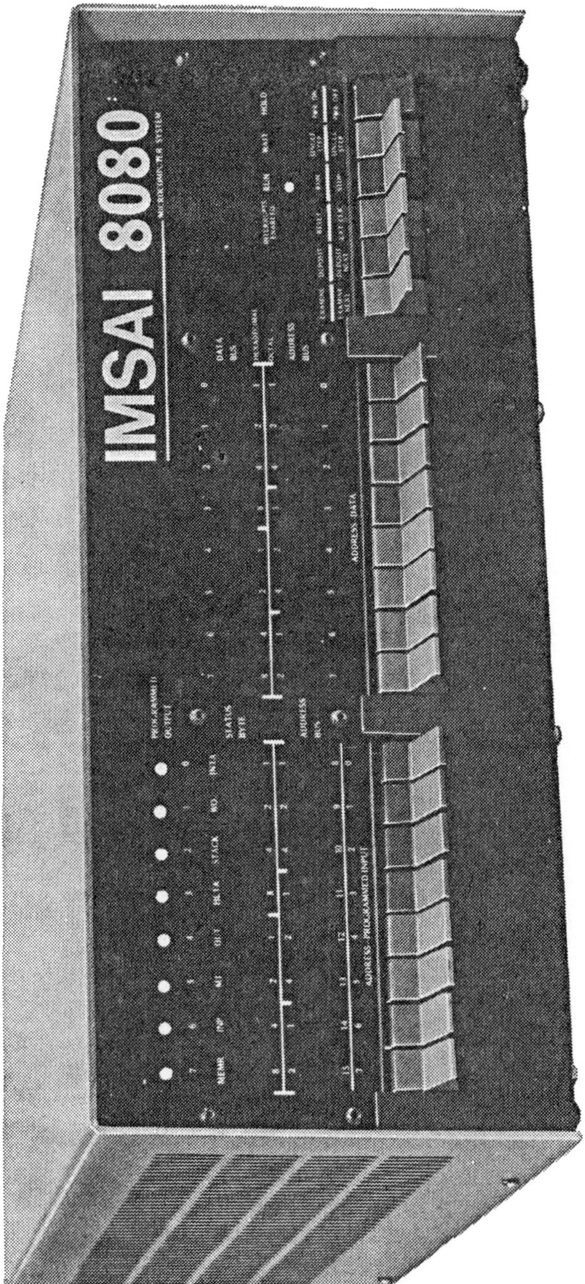

Imsai 8080

Imsai 8048

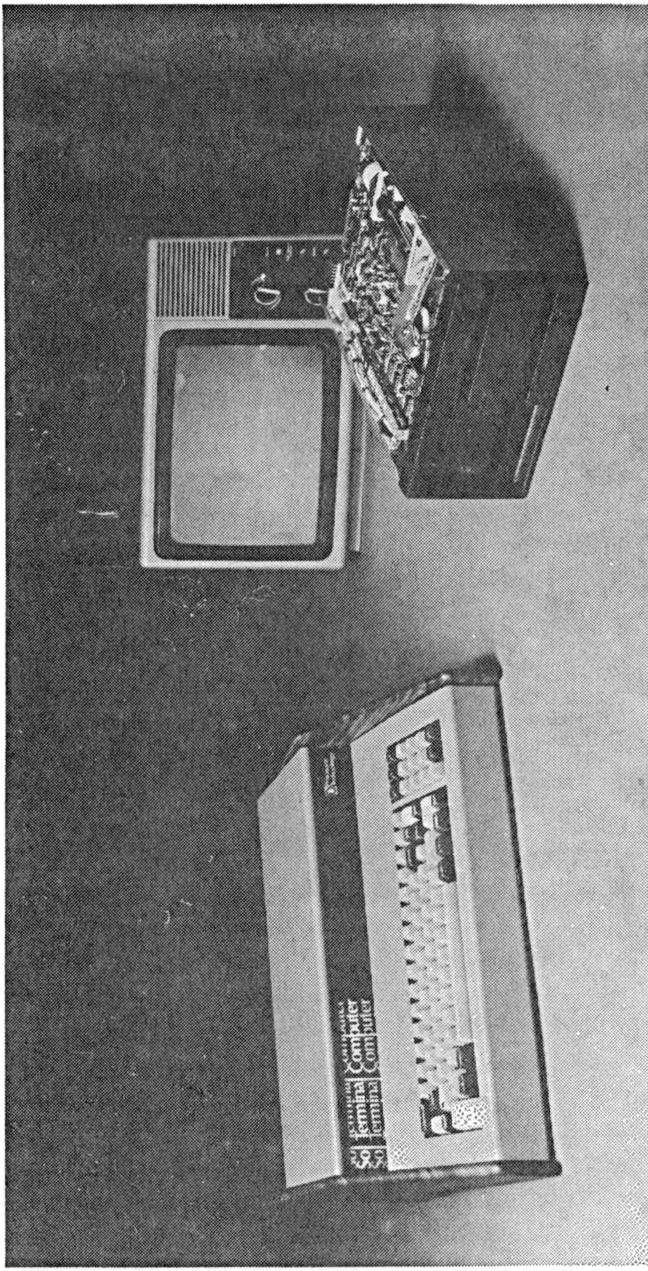

Sol

plugged into the Altair bus and puts them on a single (but rather large) PC board.

The basic Sol contains a 8080 microprocessor, a complete video processing system (with its own memory) capable of both upper-and lower-case alphanumerics, a built-in PROM operating system that does everything a front panel full of switches can do, a full keyboard, an audio cassette interface (both input and output), parallel and serial I/O ports, and a power supply that can support the Sol and up to five plug-ins of the Altair-bus variety. Sol also has a built-in extender board for servicing suspect plug-in boards. All the external connections to the Sol are via rear-apron connectors.

Sol is low profiled because the bus structure runs vertically (up from the bottom-mounted PC board). The vertically mounted bus board allows as many as five plug-ins to be made horizontally (one above the other like layers of plates). The built-in extender connector is formed by the top of the bus board.

To use Sol all you need do is connect up a CRT monitor and start Sol up. The operating system does the rest. Because it has the S-100 structure, Sol will accept a wide variety of plug-ins.

OTHER COMPUTERS ON THE BUS LINE

The Poly-88 System

PolyMorphic Systems has produced one of the most interesting computers, using the Altair/S-100 bus. It packs a lot of computing power into a small cabinet and adds video output, data I/O, and a cassette interface to communicate with the outside world. The chassis of the Poly-88 holds five circuit boards and mini-cards for the serial I/O and cassette interface. The power supply is more than enough for the cards that can be plugged into the mother board. Poly has not ended the expansion capability at five slots, for a standard edge connector has been installed in one side of the cabinet and a set of card fingers on the other. This allows the user to plug another Poly-88 into the system when required. The side-mounted edge connector is really handy for trouble shooting circuit boards as well as system expansion.

The video interface card is a self-contained interface unit because it has an input port for a keyboard. The video output is 16 lines, with as many as 64 characters or graphics on a 48 x 128 grid. Because the video uses the processor's memory, the display can be changed in less than 20 milliseconds. Other features, such as vectored interrupts and a real-time clock, are included in the Poly hardware.

The Poly-88 has just two switches. One is for power and the other is for system reset. That is all there is to control the computer. The secret of the elimination of the front panel with its banks of lights and switches lies in the monitor program on the CPU board. This ROM enables the user to control the computor at his keyboard and perform all the front-panel functions while watching the results on the video screen instead of having to interpret the LED indications. If you observe most Altair or IMSAI users you will find that they operate their computers from a terminal in exactly the same manner and rarely use the flashing lights and rows of switches. This little computer has proved to be popular with hobbyists and users in the fields of science and education. It provides portable computing power where it is needed and in an uncomplicated way.

The software support for any computer is a large factor in the selection of a machine. PolyMorphic Systems has now provided a full 8K BASIC with character and byte manipulation.

This high-level language is designed for the computer and is therefore video-display oriented. It allows the user to program graphics as well as text and arithmetic operations.

The Poly-88 costs less than other computers with the same capabilities because the buyer is not paying for the front panel he will seldom use and is buying power only for the cards he has in the machine. The Poly-88 is not for everyone, but it can be the most cost-effective answer for those who know what they want to do with a computer.

The Vector 1 Computer

Vector Graphics' Vector 1 is a new machine that includes a lot of the features of other computers and an element of flexibility that none on the market has at this time. The people at Vector Graphics do not try to capture the user for their equipment; they are willing to provide just as much, or as little, as the user wants; for example, they employ the 8080A microprocessor, but if you prefer the Z80 they will sell you one of their machines without the CPU board and not charge you for something you do not want!

Physically, the Vector 1 is a nice machine to look at. It has only one pushbutton on the front panel for system reset (the power switch is on the rear panel for safety) and comes in a choice of two colors, a touch provided by the women who run the company. If you doubt that women can run a computer company, the Vector 1 should make you think some more. They have produced one of the best built units on the market. It has a heavy clamshell cabinet, a 15-slot mother board, and a powerful power supply. Inside, the circuit cards are held by a rigid card frame and the design includes a fan for cooling the operating machine. The Vector has a CPU board, a mother board with six connectors, the cabinet and power supply, and a PROM/RAM board. This board contains the system monitor and 1K of RAM, and the firmware provided includes several options for use of IMSAI, MITS, Processor Technology, or Poly-88 output boards. This flexible arrangement means that anyone's software will run on the Vector 1.

In addition, you can buy the Vector 1 without the CPU and PROM/RAM and install a Z80 and system monitor board designed to run with it. The rest of the Vector 1 can be filled with the excellent and inexpensive Vector Graphic memory boards that have proved to be so reliable.

The Morrow CPU/Front Panel and Equinox 100

George Morrow, one of the most accomplished designers in the microcomputer field, has developed a combination 8080 CPU board for the Altair/S-100 bus and a front panel. This unit forms the basis of a user-designed computer made from stock parts. The board has a set of pushbutton switches and LED indicators that enable the user to operate the computer from a simplified front panel. It also has a monitor program on a ROM and the 8080 CPU. The board looks larger than the normal S-100 bus CPU, but it is designed to go into the bus. On closer examination the board is the size of the IMSAI front panel and the connector fingers are located so that the board will fit into an IMSAI MPU and the front panel! George Morrow, however, has designed a mother board whose unique feature is a ground line between each signal line for isolation. This board completes this designer's set of boards and constitutes a complete computer called the Equinox 100. His other designs are his excellent cassette interface, I/O, and memory boards.

Z80 CPUs AND COMPUTERS

The Z80 Microprocessor

Zilog Inc. has produced a microprocessor that in many respects is an improvement on the 8080 and 6800 chips. The personal computer industry has incorporated it into CPUs for the existing bus systems and designed a few computers to feature it. It has 158 instructions in place of the 78 used by the 8080 and includes all those of the 8080; therefore 8080 software can be adapted by the Z80. It also has more registers and needs only a single voltage level and clock rate; the 8080 requires several. The Z80 also has a lot of other improvements that affect hardware and software development. It has been called a third-generation processor. If all this is true, why not drop all the other CPUs and change to the Z80? Well, neither MITS nor IMSAI nor Processor Technology has come out with a Z80 computer, although MITS has announced a forthcoming Z80 CPU. The only manufacturers of 8080 equipment to release a Z80 system are Cromemco and the Digital Group.

Technical Design Laboratories (TDL) ZPU

TDL, located far from the source of microprocessors in Silicon Valley, California, have become the leader in Z80 software development. They produce an excellent CPU for the Altair/ S-100 bus machines, fast memory boards to run with the faster Z80, and will soon ship a system monitor board and a mother board with a power supply. These new boards will constitute the TDL XITAN Z80 System. Although it is claimed that 8080 software will run on the Z80, early revisions of Altair BASIC will not run without patches. The use of 8080 software on the Z80, however, defeats the purpose of the new chip; new software is required to follow the new instructions. TDL has a Z80 BASIC and an Editor-Assembler, recently released, and is working on additional software for the new chip. Work on a FORTRAN IV Compiler, Basic Compiler, and a more sophisticated Text Editor is now in progress at TDL.

In order to take advantage of the extra speed of the Z80, the computer must be equipped with memory that has access speeds of no more than 250 microseconds. To this end TDL produces their fast memory boards. One innovation has been to sell the Z-series of memory boards with any requested chip population. The user can later upgrade the Z8K to a Z16K by adding the extra chips. This feature plus their speed has quickly made these boards the most sought after in the industry.

TDL also offers a system monitor board which is a combination of a ROM board with monitor firmware and an I/O board. In addition, they promise a mother board and power supply combination. The sum of the TDL products will result in a powerful Z80 computer supported with software.

Cromemco Z1 and Z2

Cromemco, one of the most advanced manufacturers of boards for the S-100 bus, produced a Z80 MPU board with chips selected for 4-MHz operation. This is twice as fast as the 8080 and its use will permit the ultra-high-speed operation of personal computers as soon as memory and I/O speed catch up with the processors. Cromemco had never produced a complete computer, but it has adapted the IMSAI-8080 chassis to produce the Z1 as the first complete computer for the Z80. It followed this with the Z2, a new unit designed for dedicated programmed for a specific task applications and mounts in a standard 19-inch rack or in a table-top cabinet. The Z2 uses Cromemco 3K Control BASIC for its higher level control language.

In addition to the Z1 and Z2, this company has sold many of its Z80 MPUs for installation in Altairs, IMSAIs, and Vector ls.

The Quay Corporation

The Quay Corporation, located in New Jersey, has a S-100 bus microcomputer that gathers together the Z80 MPU, I/O, and some memory all in one unit. This can also be used for the implementation of a Z80 computer on a board that is an S-100 bus computer but can be externally connected. Quay also promises a lot of software designed for the Z80.

Other Z80 Machines

It should not be implied that S-100 bus computers are the only ones that use the Z80. Digital Group and several other manufacturers have produced Z80 computers, and OSI has included the Z80 among the microprocessors on its multiprocessor board. Wave Mate has a Z80 version of its wire-wrapped computer and several others are in the design stage.

NORTH STAR HORIZON

This new Z80-based computer from North Star Computers features their popular microdisk system and efficient BASIC. Horizon operates at 4 MHz and comes with 16K of RAM. Horizon can load or save a 10K byte disk program in less than two seconds. North Star supplies fully extended disk BASIC (including sequential and random disk files), formatted output, and a line editor.

SEALS PUP-1

Seals Electronics, well known for high quality memory products, has developed a Z80 based computer that includes dual floppies. The Peripheral Universal Processor (PUP) comes with 32K of memory, dual Shugart minifloppies, and an interface board with two serial and two parallel ports. Software for the PUP-1 includes DOS, extended BASIC and diagnostic programs. FORTRAN also will be available for this machine. The power supply will operate on electric current anywhere in the world from 90 to 260 volts ac and at 50/60 Hz.

8 6800 Systems

The Motorola 6800 Microprocessor is one of the most popular chips used to build personal computers. It offers some advantages over other processors because of its internal construction and it is simpler to program in its machine level language. The 6800 is also one of a family of chips that performs all the functions of the computer. This chapter discusses several computers based on the 6800 family and the supporting peripherals needed to make a complete system.

SWTPC 6800 SYSTEM

The Southwest Technical Products Corporation (SWTPC)

SWTPC has produced its 6800 system from proved designs and has provided a low-cost, reliable system that is popular with hobbyists, educators, and commercial users. The basic kit is derived from the design of the Motorola Evaluation Kit and uses the chip set specified for that design. The MIKBUG operating system on a ROM is included.

SWTPC has taken this design and packaged it as a set of circuit boards that plugs into a mother board. It has provided an excellent power supply, 4K of fast memory, an output board, and an attractive cabinet. The system is capable of expansion at low cost, and the circuit boards are designed with a low density of chips, which makes the unit one of the easiest computer kits to build. The kit contains all of the mother-board connectors. This represents a saving to the user because other systems charge extra for these connectors. SWTPC does not provide IC sockets with its kit and does not recommend them. Many users, however, differ on this point and do use sockets. The kit comes with excellent documentation for each of the components but is a little skimpy in instructions for interconnecting all the units into a working system.

The control I/O board supplied with the computer is designed to talk to a Teletype or a video terminal that looks like a TTY (teletypewriter) to the computer. SWTPC makes a low-cost TV typewriter for this purpose.

Software support for the SWTPC 6800 is excellent. Robert Uiterwick has written BASIC software for almost any size of memory installed. He has produced Micro-BASIC for the 4K machine, 4K BASIC for a machine with one expansion memory board, and an excellent 8K BASIC. Mr. Uiterwick will also supply the Extended Disk BASIC for SWTPC and several other 6800-based disk systems.

Additional memory boards are available from SWTPC for $100 per 4K and 8K memory boards sell for $250. Additional I/O boards are available in serial or parallel form for only $35! Several other companies have designed components for the SWTPC 6800. Smoke Signal Broadcasting Company of California has produced an excellent 16K memory and has several other products, including a low-cost disk system, on the fire. Midwest Scientific Instruments (MSI) also has many products for the 6800, including a full-sized disk and an EPROM board. Seals Electronics has a fast, low-powered memory (8K) for the

Southwest Technical Products CT-64 Terminal

SWTPC 6800. This is a version of their fine S-100 bus memory board. Beacause of this industry support, the user may be sure that his computer will not become obsolete over the next few years.

The SWTPC mother board and cabinet originally supported an expansion to 16K of memory in the cabinet. SWTPC then started to supply low-power chips and the capacity went up to 20K. Now that 8K and even 16K boards are available, the computer can use up to 48K of memory in the chassis. It should be noted that although the microprocessor has 16 address lines and should be able to address up to 64K of memory some of it is taken up by the operating system on ROM. Because 6800 uses memory mapping for output ports, somewhat less memory is available for RAM. This memory mapping is one of the differences between the 6800 and 8080 microprocessors. In the 6800 each output port is a location in memory, addressed just as if it were a memory board. A look at the memory map for a 6800 computer will show where each peripheral is located. This use of memory locations would seem to restrict the memory capacity of the computer; however, a scheme to get around this is called restriction. Additional memory is organized in blocks and each block is addressed as one memory location! This scheme permits expansion of the memory to megabytes! It has not yet been used in the SWTPC 6800 but it can be done. Southwest Technical will also sell extra chassis, power supplies, and mother boards for expansion beyond the original cabinet.

CT-64

The TVT, which is a low-cost video terminal, was the original SWTPC computer product. In fact, an earlier version of the first TV typewriter by Don Lancaster was the first home computer design reproduced in a magazine.

Thousands of these Southwest terminals have been built and are in service. They represent the cheapest way to interface to a computer and obtain alphanumeric readout on a CRT screen. The CT-64 is also being used for time sharing by countless students who find it the only way to get time on a school computer. The CT-1024 has some limitations: first, it has only 64 characters per 16 lines of display area; second, it has only upper case characters and does not scroll on the screen. These limitations have been overcome, and Southwest Technical Products is replacing the unit with a new terminal that contains everything the CT-1024 lacks, including a case! The keyboard for the CT-1024 is known as the KBD-5. It will be used in the new terminal and is available as a separate keyboard for use with other computers

The AC-30 Cassette Interface

This mass storage device converts digital data into audio tones and connects to an ordinary audio cassette recorder which enters the data on tape. It plays back by reading the tape, converts the audio to digital data, and inputs it to the computer.

SWTPC designed the AC-30 as a free-standing unit rather than as a plug-in to the computer or video terminal. It has its own power supply and cabinet with control panel. It can be used with a cassette recorder of reasonable quality and operates on the "Kansas City standard" of 300-baud.

This standard was agreed to by several manufacturers in an attempt to regulate the many conflicting tape-recording systems in use.

When the AC-30 is used with the SWTPC 6800 and CT-64, it can be installed between them. This eliminates the need for a separate interface for the cassette unit.

Independent control circuits are provided for two audio cassette recorders. The tape from one can be read while the other unit is recording data. The operating mode for each recorder is selected by switches on the front panel and LED indicator lights show the mode selected at the time. Computer-controlled

RECORD and PLAY and motor-controlled commands can be used if they are available from the terminal. (The CT-1024 has this feature if the CT-CA cursor control is installed.)

It should be noted that the AC-30 is an *interface,* not a tape controller. The difference is not always understood by the hobbyists. An interface converts data into recordable form and transmits them to a recording device. It also reads tone signals from a tape and converts them into digital data. The AC-30 can start and stop the tape drive motor if the recorder is equipped with a remote microphone control relay.

A tape controller does all that an interface can do, but it has, in addition, the ability to drive a cassette recorder (equipped with two motors) in both directions and to search the tape for a specified block of data under software control. It can also read a list (header) at the start of the tape and remember the location of the various files. The AC-30 is not such a device. This feature is found only in high-cost digital-type recording systems.

PR-40 Printer

One of the drawbacks of a video-based computer system is the lack of printed "hard copy" which is often required for permanent records. Teletype printing terminals and line printers usually cost more than the rest of a small computer system. One exception is the SWTPC PR-40 printer, which costs only $250 in kit form. The printer mechanism comes completely built and the user builds only the electronics and assembles the base. The PR-40 is a dot-matrix, 75-line-per-minute printer with a 64-character ASCII character set. It also has a 40-character line buffer which means that the printer accepts 40 characters and then prints a line. It can also decode the character for carriage return; when a short line is terminated by this character, it causes the printer to print.

The PR-40 uses ordinary 3 7/8-inch adding machine paper obtainable in most office supply stores. However, the 5/16-inch ribbons are not easy to find. They can be respooled from 5/16-inch typewriter ribbons, but this is messy. The printer is made for intermittent duty, which means that if it is operated for a considerable time it will burn out the solenoids that fire the printing needles. This can be overcome by setting the printer for light printing and putting cooling heat sinks on the solenoids. The best remedy is prevention. Use the printer to print only the data you need in permanent form.

The PR-40 printer is also adaptable to other computer systems and is finding wide acceptance.

The reader will notice other printers advertised that look a great deal like the SWTPC PR-40 but priced higher. Investigation will show that these are the same mechanisms with slightly more complex circuits to print in both directions or with a slightly longer line length.

GT-61 Video Graphics Terminal

This kit permits the user to add video graphics to a personal computing system. It is a self-contained device with its own memory space. The theory of the graphics board is a little beyond the beginner, but it produces graphic designs on a video screen by having the computer write dots on the screen under program control.

The basic SWTPC kit contains a circuit board with all the necessary components, but it does not include a cabinet or power supply. Southwest Technical Products also has produced a set of joystick controls to enable the user to play video games with the videographics terminal.

ALTAIR 680b

The Altair 680b is the tiny brother of the Altair 8800 but it is a powerful 6800 computer when it is equipped with enough memory. The 680b differs from other 6800 machines because it has a complete set of front-panel switches that can be used to enter programs and a set of LED indicators to show program entry and results. The 680b is essentially a one-board computer mounted in a case and equipped with a front panel and power supply. Provision is also made to mount three additional circuit boards. This gives the 680b expansion capability to become a complete 6800 computer system. MITS has designed a 16K memory board to give the 680b extra memory in one plug-in. They have also written a version of their powerful BASIC to run on the 680b when it is equipped with the extra memory board. The other two available slots can also be used for memory or I/O boards. I/O is available for the 680b to interface it to a great variety of terminals, from a five-level Baudot Teletype to a modern video terminal. The unit is easy to construct and comes with MITS excellent documentation.

For those who plan to build the Altair 680b and want a higher level language without the expense of the 16K memory MITS has developed VTL or very tiny language. This will run in the 1K of memory that is on the basic computer. Although it is not a powerful computer language, it is interesting as a development tool and as a way of using an unexpanded Altair 680b.

WAVE MATE JUPITER II SYSTEM

The Jupiter II is an unusual 6800 system that departs from the methods of construction found in most personal computers and uses wire-wrapped circuit modules. This method of construction, when correctly done, produces an electronic assembly of high reliability and low rate of failure. Wave Mate has enclosed the unit in a sturdy card cage and provided a front-panel unit mounted behind a plexiglass panel. The controls are three operation switches and a four-digit hex display of the system address bus. The functions provided are System Reset, Front Panel Interrupt, Run/Halt, and Single Step Instruction. One status light

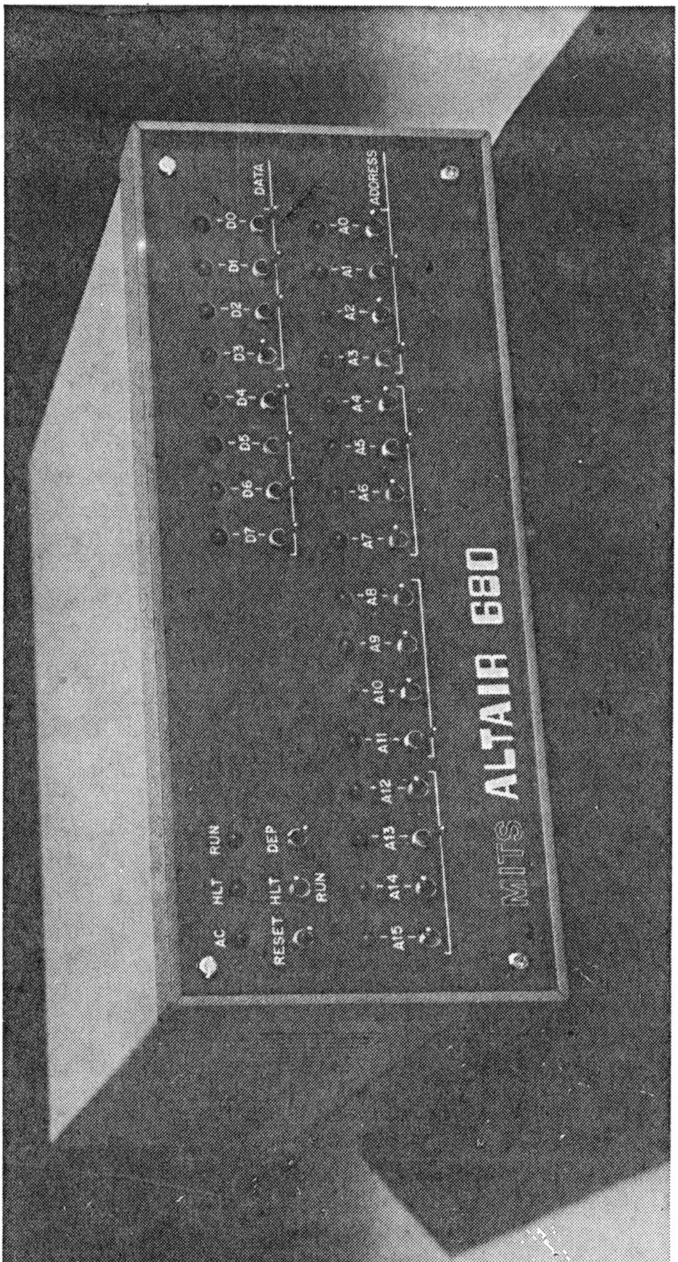
MITS ALTAIR 680
AC HLT RUN
RESET HLT DEP
RUN
A15 A14 A13 A12 A11 A10 A9 A8
D7 D6 D5 D4 D3 D2 D1 D0
DATA
A7 A6 A5 A4 A3 A2 A1 A0
ADDRESS

Altair 680b

displays the Run/Halt status of the 6800 processor and any DMA (direct memory address) activity on the system bus. A second light shows the amount of interrupt processing in the CPU unit.

The system has a software monitor and debugger program in EPROMS, designed to match the I/O configuration of the user's system. The firmware is supplied in a module that includes an address breakpoint comparator and single-step routines. These are useful in debugging programs. The module also has a small amount of "scratch pad" memory to work with the EPROMS.

The system power supply is modular and plugs into the card cage, leaving eight slots for system modules. If additional module slots are required to configure a system, an expansion module cage is available with its own power supply.

The system can include dynamic RAM memory, static RAM memory, or EPROM memory modules. To promote system development an EPROM programmer module is provided. It will program EPROMs right in the computer.

Wave Mate produces interface modules for serial data or parallcl data. Both singlc and dual vcrsions arc availablc. To usc the system as a versatile hardware development tool prototype modules and additional voltage kits for the power supply are available.

The manufacturer has also provided excellent software support, including assembler and 8K BASIC.

A full line of peripherals to match the Jupiter II is sold by Wave Mate. It contains a dual audio cassette interface module, a video display module, an ASCII keyboard, and a 12-inch video monitor.

The Jupiter II System is constructed in accordance with the best commercial computer practice and configured for extensive system development. It may seem to be a case of overkill for most hobbyists, but for those who are interested in serious computer experiments this system will be attractive. The total cost does not

9 The Digital Group

The system philosophy of The Digital Group is opposed to the rigid structure imposed by the Altair/IMSAI S-100 bus design. The very standardization that has permitted development of many devices for that bus system has excluded use of microprocessors that do not conform to the requirements of the 8080-type processor.

The Digital Group believes that the only consistent element in the field of personal computing is change. The investment of time and money in a computer system is large and should not be expended on one that may become out of date in a short time.

The Digital Group believes that a personal computing system should be capable of adapting to the changes brought on by the introduction of newer, faster, and better microprocessors. Otherwise the frustrated system-owner will be stuck with obsolete equipment.

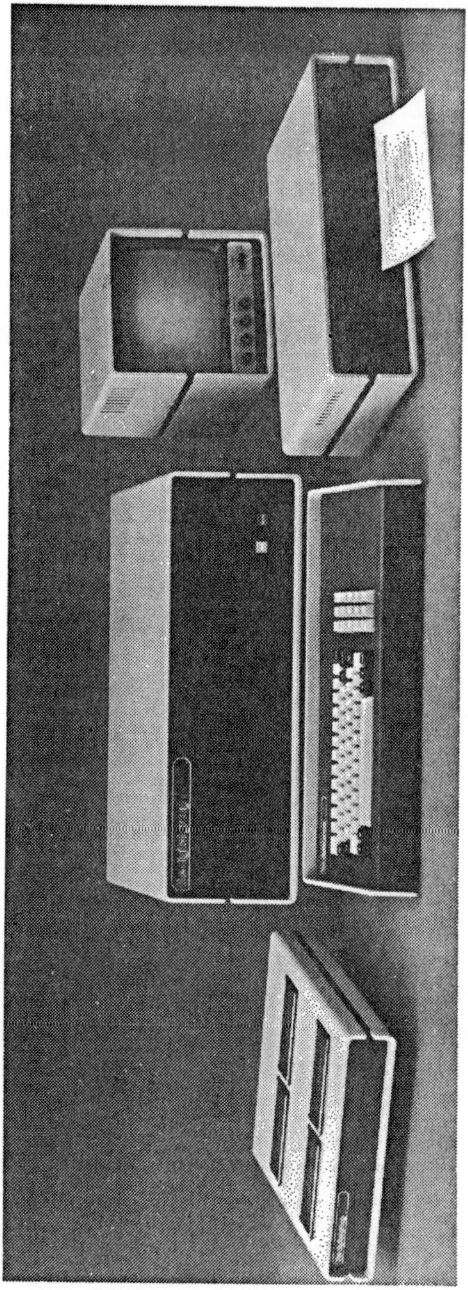

The Digital Group System

THERE ARE OTHER BUS ROUTES

The Digital Group system is designed to adjust to change because compatability of the system is maintained no matter which microprocessor board is used. All memory, input/output, and peripherals are completely independent of the MPU board selected. At this time the Digital Group offers MPU boards that use any of the following processors:

Intel/AMD/Nec 8080
Motorola 6800
Zilog/Mostek Z80
MOS Technology 6502

With a Digital Group system the user can change from an 8080 MPU to a 6800 MPU by unplugging the 8080 card and plugging in the 6800 card! When the power is turned on and the 6800 operating system cassette is loaded, the user has switched from an 8080 to a 6800 system. The same is true of the 6502. With the advent of the new Z80, The Digital Group was one of the first manufacturers to offer this advanced processor. Because the Z80 offers most of the major advantages of the 8080, 6800, and 6500 processors, plus 80 additional new instructions and increased speed, The Digital Group has enabled their users to upgrade with a minimum of trouble and cost. For new purchasers the cost of a Z80 is only $50 more than the 8080 price.

Another aspect of The Digital Group system is their concentration on a video-based personal computer system, the reason for which is that they consider that a system based on toggle-switches and LED readouts is unsatisfactory because it presents the user with only one character and one address at a time. This byte-by-byte readout is not useful to meaningful computation. Teletype and other expensive terminal-based I/O systems take system cost and complexity beyond the range of the average user. Old surplus teletypes are noisy, difficult to interface, and unreliable. Old video terminals are prone to trouble and are usually no longer supported by the manufacturers.

The Digital Group alternative to the I/O problem has been the design of a video-based system which has cassette mass storage of operating system, application programs, and data. A converted TV set, or an inexpensive monitor, is used as the display, an alphanumeric keyboard is the input, and an ordinary audio cassette is the mass storage device. The system is silent and almost instantaneous.

The Digital Group system requires no front panel. The instructions to start-up are contained in an EPROM bootstrap loader. Loading or changing of memory is accomplished by two major TV-oriented functions: keyboard program and storage dump. Each of these functions may be called from the other.

It should be noted that this system differs from the SWTPC 6800 system in that the SWTPC 6800 uses an operating system called MIKBUG that is entirely in PROM, whereas in The Digital Group system only the bootstrap loader is on EPROM. The operating system itself is on a cassette. This means that although the loading program is constant the operating program can change from processor to processor. A typical operating system has the following types of function:

1. Read cassette.
2. Write cassette.
3. Program from the keyboard.
4. Dump storage.
5. TV monitor functional support routines.

Functions 3, 4, and 5 are supplied in octal or hexadecimal notation, depending on the processor selected. Initial operations on any Digital Group system are simple:

1. Load a system cassette, program cassette into the cassette player, and press PLAY.

2. Turn on the computer power.
3. When the contents of the cassette are read into the computer, a list will appear on the video screen. This list will display an application for each application program on the tape.
4. Select an application code and type it in by means of the keyboard. The application will start.

System Software and Support

In addition to the operating systems for each microprocessor, The Digital Group has supported their systems with large quantities of software. Their excellent system maintenance routines include an effective memory check program. BASIC is available in several versions: Tiny BASIC, Tiny BASIC Extended and Maxi-BASIC, all of which provide a high-level language for any memories of any size.

The Digital Group also has a separate division devoted to software development. This division called Digital Group Software Systems is now packaging games and other useful applications for the users of The Digital Group system. Independent software firms are writing business applications and business packages using The Digital Group system supported by several of the group's dealers will soon be on the market.

It should be noted that Digital Group equipment and software are sold and serviced by a growing network of dealers throughout the United States and Europe.

What Are the Disadvantages of The Digital Group System?

If The Digital Group system has so many unique and desirable features, why isn't it the leading personal computing system? Well, to many technically knowledgeable hobbyists it is the leading system. To the uninformed newcomer, however, the system looks strange. It does not use the familar Altair/IMSAI S-100 bus structure, and the design of each type of card is somewhat different. Cabinets to house the system have only recently appeared, but they are very attractive and will do a lot to raise the standing of the system. A user is restricted to equipment made by The Digital Group and must pass up the goodies made for the Altair bus.

The Phi-Deck Mass Storage System from The Digital Group

Most cassette data storage systems used in hobbyist computer systems are designed to operate with inexpensive audio cassette recorders by converting the 1s and 0s in the data stream into two audio tones and then recording them on ordinary Phillips-type audio cassettes. When reading, the tape recorder plays the tones and the cassette interface recreates the data in a form that the computer will understand. It is unlike the digital tape systems used by the large computer systems.

Many of the cassette recorders are not precise in speed or head spacing and interchange among users is not easy. The greatest fault is that the ordinary cassette recorder can move in only one direction until it is stopped and the reverse pushbutton is manually pushed. No tape search for specific data blocks can be made under these conditions.

The Phi-Deck digital cassette is a true digital cassette drive that records the data in direct digital form. It does, however, use Phillips-type cassettes that pack a far greater amount of data on the tape. The Phi-Deck drive moves the tape back and forth under motor control. Electronic braking controls the tapes precisely for fast forward, rewind, and search operations. File systems can be implemented with this system and data searched for and read in rapid order.

The Digital Group has developed a controller for the Phi-Deck which will operate as many as four drives and access any of the more than one-quarter million 8-bit bytes in a random access time of 20 seconds, using Phillips-type C-30 cassettes. This has proved to be one of the most effective low-cost mass-storage data devices available. Many users of other computer systems have tried to interface it to their units. Its availability is a definite plus for The Digital Group.

The Digital Group Printer

The Digital Group technology has now filled one of the gaps in the personal computer system. Until recently there has been no printer with a full page width at a reasonable price. The cost of printers exceeded the total cost of many complete computer systems. The Digital Group printer fills the need with a fast 120-characters-per-second, 96-characters-per-line impact matrix printer for less than $500 (less than the cost of a used ASR-33 teletypewriter!). This printer uses standard 8 1/2-inch paper and can make four copies at one time. The printer is software driven and can do some interesting things, such as varying the character set and pitch to make it possible to print 132 characters at 16 pitch or to print double-width characters. These are features now found only on very expensive machines. Most interesting is the fact that the printer can be interfaced to existing I/O ports on any bus structure. Thus The Digital Group has not only filled the need for hard copy on their own system but has provided a product that all personal computers can use.

10 Other Systems to Consider

Just one year ago the number of personal computers on the market could be counted on one hand and the buyer had only a few factors to consider before making a choice. Today the choice is much wider, and in a short time the public will be offered hundreds of models, each of which will feature some advantage. The buyer must consider them all before settling on a machine. The following paragraphs cover the equipment already for sale or about to be released at the time of publication. The reader should also consider the merits of any new equipment that reaches the market after publication of this book.

OHIO SCIENTIFIC INSTRUMENTS AND THE CHALLENGER

Ohio Scientific Instruments (OSI) is a company in a college town far from the center of computer manufacture in Silicon

Valley and the northeast coast. Perhaps that is why it and its leader Mike Cheiky have developed some unusual ideas for the computer hobbyist and educational user. OSI first developed the Series 400 superboard, which is a microprocessor board with the capability of becoming a one-board computer or the CPU of a powerful computer system. In addition, the superboard can be equipped with a Motorola 6800 or a MOS Technology 6502 microprocessor. The user can add extra RAM, ROM, and all kinds of I/O capability. When the hobbyist has advanced to the point of expansion to a complete system, OSI provides a complete backplane, power supply, and cabinet. A full complement of cassette interfaces, memory, videographics, and I/O boards, and even a floppy-disk system can be installed. In all, OSI offers the greatest flexibility possible.

The most interesting feature of the OSI system is the availability of its components in increments that permit the hobbyist to proceed at his own pace and ability to pay.

First, the boards are "bare boards" complete with documentation, but that's all! The price for most of them is only $29 or $39! OSI will also provide "hard-to-get parts" at low volume cost. Boards can also be purchased as a complete kit. The latest development is the OSI Challenger, completely factory-built. This unit is the lowest priced, fully expandable, completely assembled computer on the market. It is supported with Extended BASIC for the M6800 and 6502 versions. OSI will supply the Challenger as a video computer or a Teletype I/O version. BASIC is available, free of charge, to users who buy enough memory to use it. BASIC can also be had at a low cost by those who are building their own systems. OSI is also providing one of the lowest cost floppy-disk systems available for both the 6800 and 6502.

There are some drawbacks to doing business with OSI. The company is small and it is sometimes hard to get in touch with them. Shipments are slow at times, and it is not easy to get all the parts for the "bare-bones" kits. The biggest problem is the documentation, which is still not in finished form. The effort is worthwhile, however, because the value is great compared with that offered on the present market. More computer stores are now carrying the line and distribution problems are expected to clear up soon.

OSI's most interesting idea is its CPU expander board, a unit that permits the use of multiprocessors in the computer! The 6100 (which runs DEC PDP-8 software), Z80, and other new processors on the way can all be used in the OSI Computer equipped with a CPU expander.

It is interesting to note that the 6502 remains in the machine to act as host processor, an idea borrowed from the largest machines. Even though it is one of the smaller computer manufacturers, OSI should be considered in your plans for a personal computer.

THE COMPUCOLOR 8001 COMPUTER

Intelligent Systems Corporation has produced a version of their color CRT terminal with options that make it a complete 8080A-based color computer. This unit is unique in that it operates with color graphics and has its high-level BASIC in PROMs. There is nothing like it in the field of personal computing and it adds a new dimension to all computer display.

The Compucolor 8001 is completely constructed and tested. It has a powerful BASIC with color-graphic plotting commands and an 8080 operating CRT system. Options are provided to install a light pen for graphic generation and for additional memory and editing capabilities. The unit comes with 8K BASIC on PROMs, a 3K operating system for the 8080, 8K of memory for the color operation of the CRT, and 8K of user RAM. Additional memory expansion of 24K of user RAM and 10K of ROM is provided for.

An interesting component of Compucolor is the tape mass-storage system called a floppy tape. It is an eight-track cartridge-tape system that can load or save programs under program control exactly like a floppy disk, except for the access speed and use of tape cartridges. Tapes are available for storage of 72K bytes to 1M byte. A single floppy tape unit is available for other computers for only $250, one quarter of the price of the cheapest floppy-disk system. The Compucolor is finding broad applications in business and video-graphics, where color-graphic capabilities are desired. Reports, graphs, and balance sheets are improved by the use of color graphics from the computer. A conventional micro-floppy disk is also available for the 8001.

APPLE I COMPUTER

Apple 1 is a one-board, 6502-based computer sold as a constructed unit. The board contains an input section with a connector for a full keyboard and a video display section with composite video output to a monitor. The Apple 1 is supplied with 4K of memory and provides for plugging in additional memory. The power supply, with the exception of the transformers, which are available locally for a few dollars, is also installed on the board.

A connector at one end provides installation for the audio cassette board, which is fast and reliable and operates with almost any cassette unit. A set of connector "fingers" at the edge of the board allows for future expansion, although no additional boards had been released at the time of this writing.

Apple Computer has produced some of the best software written for the 6502 microprocessor. Their BASIC has many features not found in versions that run in a lot more memory! The Apple crew has also written games and machine-language subroutines for the 6502 which extend the usability of the unit.

The only worm in the Apple 1 is its inability to expand the unit physically into a full system. Apple has not yet delivered the promised expansion boards for I/O and memory; however, they plan to replace the 4K memory chips with 16K memory chips.

APPLE II COMPUTER

One of the first of the "magic-box" personal computers, the Apple II made its appearance in the spring of 1977. It is a big improvement over the original Apple computer, for it features the one-board computer with expansion capabilities, an attractive case and keyboard, and expandable memory. Apple II will also operate in color, monitored by a home color TV. It comes with excellent software and is easy to use. To those who are willing to spend more than a thousand dollars Apple II offers a lot in a small package. It has been around long enough to have the "bugs" ironed out and therefore should be popular with people who are waiting for their own personal computers but do not want to build one. Because the market for home computers will demand ready-built machines, Apple II will be in the forefront as a supplier of personal computers for other buyers than the dedicated hobbyist. Supported by Apple BASIC and color, this machine will be hard to beat.

PET COMPUTER

This personal computer was the first shown to the public at the San Francisco Computer Fair in 1977 and was described as the first low-cost complete personal computer. The Pet (Personal Electronics Transacter) is the entry of Commodore Business Machines Corporation, one of the big producers of low-cost calculators. Having observed the explosion of interest in home computers, Commodore acquired MOS Technology, a manufacturer of microprocessors, notably the 6500 family. MOS Technology had already produced the KIM-1, a computer-on-a-board widely used by original equipment manufacturers and sold direct to many hobbyists. KIM-1 sold for $245 and was popular as an inexpensive entry in the computer hobby field. MOS Technology provided neither extensive software support nor inexpensive expansion capability for the KIM-1, and many hobbyists, having learned about computers from their KIM-1s, switched to more complex machines. The Pet uses some of the same technology but is completely housed in a unified package, including video screen and cassette data-storage device. It is therefore the first complete packaged computer system to be made available to the general public and is planned to list for around $500. If this machine proves to be reliable and can be merchandized at a really low price, it will really spark home use of computers. It is apparent that Pet will sell far below the price of its nearest competitor, but several of the larger microcomputer manufacturers have entries in prototype ready for an expanding market. The result of the race to put a computer in every home will not be known for several years, but if the trends of the calculator industry are followed a few large firms will soon be selling many varieties of home computing machines.

THE MMD-1 DESIGNER COMPUTER

This 8080-based unit was featured in *Radio Electronics* in a construction article and is being produced by E & L Instruments, publishers of the famous Bugbooks. A special Bugbook used with this computer makes it an excellent training device as well as a software development tool.

The unit has a hex keyboard and a LED display and may be used without any other terminal. An additional board is available to provide memory additions and cassette storage capabilities. Interface to a teletypewriter is also possible. This system must be considered an educational tool, for it is incapable of being expanded into a personal computing system; it is, however, one of the best of its kind.

HAL MCEM-8080 COMPUTER

The HAL is not the evil computer in the movie 2001, but an 8080-based device built by the HAL Communications Corporation, well known in amateur radio. This one-board computer features a 1K ROM operating system with expansion to 4K, 1K of RAM with expansion to 2K, and a varied I/O capability. HAL provides TTY serial I/O, RS-232 serial I/O, and three parallel I/O ports. In addition, the MCEM-8080 can interface to a five-level baudot teletypewriter used by hams for RTTY operation. This board is supplied as a factory-built unit and has interface to HAL's DS-3000 KSR terminal, also popular with hams.

KIM-1 COMPUTER

KIM-1 is a low-cost, one-board computer made by MOS Technology, Inc., manufacturer of the 6502 microprocessor. Its chief features are its price ($245), hex keyboard, and LED display. It is also equipped with a cassette interface and a serial I/O for a Teletype. The documentation of this well-made board is excellent. The KIM-1 is a fine training device for microcomputers in general and the 6502 in particular. Problems develop when hobbyists try to expand it into a personal computer system. The expansion components are expensive and hard to find and the assembled computer is hard to package. One other drawback is the lack of software. The manufacturer has never supported the chip or the KIM with high-level software and other software developed by Apple and OSI does not run easily on the KIM. Tiny BASIC by Tom Pitman is one exception. It is possible to connect KIM to an OSI backplane and expand it with OSI boards. This route has been traveled by many users. The KIM-1 makes an excellent control computer; a robot whose brain is a KIM and many other applications in electrical control have been documented in the magazines.

NATIONAL SEMICONDUCTOR SC/MP COMPUTER

The microcomputer kit available at lowest cost is the National

Semiconductor SC/MP, popularly called the Scamp and marketed for $99. One problem, however, is that it requires a $1000 Teletype to run the $99 Scamp! National has now provided a keyboard to replace the Teletype. It is a hand-held unit the size of a pocket calculator! The Scamp has become attractive as a learning tool that can be used later for control applications and as a peripheral in a larger system. National, unlike MOS Technology, however, is supporting the Scamp with an active applications program and a users' group. They have even developed a Tiny BASIC for the little computer. Scamp plus the keyboard is a "sleeper" for those who want to get involved "a little bit." Several of the hobby magazines have run feature articles on the Scamp that should be read before you buy.

RCA COSMAC ELF COMPUTER

One of the most interesting microprocessors on the market is the RCA COSMAC or CD1802. The only hobby computer based on this chip is the Elf, plans for which were published in *Popular Electronics.* A kit version has now appeared. One microcomputer that uses the chip, the UC1800, built by Infinate Inc., has now been featured in the magazines. This little device is more of a development unit than a personal computer, but it is the first non-RCA use of the chip. The COSMAC was exhibited at the Personal Computer '76 Show in Atlantic City and much interest was expressed.

MICROMIND COMPUTER

This computer from the ECD Corporation of Cambridge, Mass., has been advertised for several months. According to the ads, the Micromind will come with a software-definable keyboard, an I/O interface, a 6500-series processor, high-detail graphics, a video display that plugs into any TV set through a coupler, and high-level BASIC. This unit can be expanded with 32K memory boards and will have a memory-mapping option that will permit expansion of the memory to 64 megabytes! The cassette interface will operate at 3200 bits per second and an ordinary tape recorder can be used!

This author attended a meeting in New York to see the Micromind, but the unit was not available at that time. By the time this book is published the units should be delivered. If they perform as advertised, they will represent a major improvement in personal computing and many other units now on the market will be obsolete. Talks with the manufacturers have indicated that the Micromind is only their initial offering and more wonders are in store!

The interesting thing about the Micromind is that the demand for advanced personal computers is so great that many have been sold sight unseen.

TRS-80 MICROCOMPUTER SYSTEM

The Tandy Corporation, parent of the Radio Shack stores, has entered the home computer market with a Z80-based computer system. The TRS-80 is a departure from conventional system architecture in that it has no card-plugable system bus.

The TRS-80 system consists of a small case mounting a 53-key ASCII keyboard and containing the Z80 microcomputer circuit board. The video display unit is a separate 12-inch CRT and the power supply is also a separate unit.

The TRS-80 comes equipped with an operating system and BASIC in 4K of ROM and an additional 4K of dynamic memory (expandable to 16K) for the user's programs. Mass storage of programs is through a separate cassette tape.

The video generation is done on the computer circuit board and is a memory-mapped display. This means that the user can display the cursor or any character anywhere on a 126-point horizontal by 48-point vertical grid. Or the user can type alphanumeric characters as 16 lines of either 32 or 64 characters. This graphic/alphanumeric capability is accomplished through the BASIC commands, and graphics can be interspersed with text by software. This feature makes the TRS-80 a powerful tool for teaching or design use. The video output is connected to the 12-inch CRT by a cable.

The power supply for the computer is UL listed for 120V ac at 60 Hz, a feature desirable for schools and institutions. Since the system is based upon the Z80 microprocessor (which requires only a single voltage) and also uses low-power dynamic RAM, the small power supply is adequate for the system. The video and tape units have their own power supplies.

The TRS-80 BASIC is remarkable for the power that has been incorporated into 4K. It has floating-point math, array and string capabilities in addition to the X-Y plotting commands.

Programs may be loaded and saved through CLOAD and CSAVE commands using a cassette recorder that operates at 500 baud (a non-standard speed). Radio Shack intends to provide owners with programmed cassettes at low cost; in fact it sees this "after market" for pre-recorded programs as one of the attractions of the home computer market.

Tandy Corporation has already announced expansion units for the TRS-80. These consist of a floppy disk and a memory expansion box. This points up the main weakness of the system. There is no expandable plug-in bus with built-in power supply. The user will be required to add boxes to expand the system and each unit will require its own power supply with a line-cord.

The 4K of user memory supplied with the TRS-80 is expandable by memory-chip upgrade. Since the computer has so many interesting and powerful capabilities, expansion through this upgrade is likely, so the TRS-80 owner soon will be back to his local Radio Shack for more memory.

To permit further expansion, the unit has an "expansion port" in the form of a card-edge with fingers. This can accept a cable connector. The user can thereby connect the memory box and floppy disk to the computer by means of a ribbon cable. Although no hard-copy device is offered at this time, a RS-232 (EIA) connector will be supplied for the future. Tandy recognizes the need for a printing device and intends to provide a low cost unit.

The TRS-80 will be marketed through Tandy Computer Stores, selected Radio Shacks and the mail order Allied Radio catalog. The introductory system price of $599 will attract a lot of people to the home computer field and provide a low-cost starter unit. A hobbyist with his own video monitor and cassette player can buy the CPU/keyboard unit for under $400.

HEATHKIT H8 AND H11

One of the latest of the "big-name" companies to enter the personal computer area, Heath has come in with two computers, a terminal, and some useful peripherals.

Their H8 Digital Computer is based on the 8080 microprocessor and features a 1K operating system in ROM, a 9-digit, 7-segment LED octal display and a 16-key keypad to gain entry into the system. The readouts can display memory contents and registers when the computer is operating. Four LED's are used as status indicators, and a built-in loudspeaker is used to produce a variety of sound effects ranging from 'end-of-line' beeps to sound effects for games.

The bus structure is unique to Heath, consists of two 25-pin connectors, and can support 10 plug-ins. The kit comes with everything but RAM memory, and Heath provides separate expandable RAM kits with 4K expansion. Among the peripherals currently available are an I/O board that also contains a 1200-baud audio interface and a three-port parallel I/O.

The companion CRT terminal, the Heath H9, features a

67-key ASCII keyboard and an 80-character by 12-line display. This terminal can be set up for four columns of 20 characters by 12 lines, full cursor control, batch transmit, and a plot (graphics) mode. The baud rate is selectable between 110 (standard TTY) and 9600 baud. I/O is either RS232 or 20-mA current loop.

Software for the H8 includes Benton Harbor BASIC, available on paper tape or audio cassette; the HASL-8 assembler; TED-8, a line-oriented text editor; and BUG-8, a terminal console debugging program. This entire package comes with the H8 kit.

If you are looking for a more powerful computer consider the Model H11. This machine is based on the well-known 16-bit Digital Equipment Corp. LST-11. The computer comes from Heath with its CPU board wired and tested and with 4K of RAM (16-bits wide). The internal memory of the H11 is expandable to 20K.

The H11 comes with DEC software that includes an editor, assembler, linker, on-line debugger, I/O executive, and BASIC and FOCAL languages. Among the available options are a 4K (by 16 bits) RAM board and a serial/parallel I/O board. Purchasers of the H11 can join the Digital Equipment Computer Users Society (DECUS) that has over 800 programs for the H11.

Another peripheral is the H10 paper tape reader and tape punch. This device uses conventional one-inch paper tape, can punch the tape at 10 characters per second, and read the tape at 50 characters per second.

BALLY LIBRARY COMPUTER

At first glance this appears to be a video game player. But a look below the surface shows many of the elements of a personal computing system.

Designed and built by Bally, the well-known manufacturer of those games seen in every "video arcade," and available from JS&A, One JS&A Plaza, Northbrook, Ill. 60062, this new home system features a Z80 microprocessor, 12K of internal memory (ROM and RAM), a keyboard, and capacity for internal sound effects. It delivers video signals for use by the conventional TV receivers. The basic cost is around $300.

For this cost you receive the computer, four pistol grips for use in game playing, an ac adapter, three arcade-type games, a calculator program, and a one-year warranty on the wired and tested assembly. Just in case a problem occurs, a self-diagnostic tape is included. High-resolution graphics is the result of using a 160 x 100 dot matrix.

Announced for the future are a baseball/paddle game tape, a math-table/math-bingo tape, a light pen, color displays and a music synthesizer. Also announced are a dual tape-deck, an alpha-numeric keyboard, 16K memory expansion, BASIC, and a high-speed printer. When the latter devices are available, the Bally will be a full-fledged personal computer.

11 Peripherals and Input/Output Devices

A digital computer is designed to do things. Somehow data must get from the outside world into the computer and out again after processing, and that is where peripherals and I/O (input/output) ports come in.

The data in the computer is generated on the eight data lines, assuming an 8-bit computer, but unfortunately all 8 bits are present on the data lines at one time. (This is called parallel data). This condition is at odds with many I/O devices such as the Teletype or video terminals that operate with serial data (one bit at a time). Therefore some means must be found to perform the necessary two-way conversion.

SERIAL I/O — THE UART

The most common way to accomplish the two-way serial to parallel and parallel to serial conversions is with a device called a

UART, short for *U*niversal *A*synchronous *R*eceiver *T*ransmitter. Essentially, this mouthful describes an IC that accepts digital data in parallel form and transmits the data in serial form. The other half of the IC receives the data from the outside world in serial form and waits until it has the complete 8-bit byte. It then dumps the complete byte in parallel form onto the computer data-bus.

This explains the meaning of receiver and transmitter, but what about "asynchronous?"

In data communications there are two basic types of serial transmission. One is called synchronous because the incoming data words are locked into the computer timing. If the timing between the computer and the serial device are not in step, garbled transmission will result. Because most computers operate rapidly and peripherals very slowly [Teletypes operate at only 110 baud (bits per second) and video terminals operate up to 9600 baud], some means must be found to get the data from the outside world in step with the computer. This is where "asynchronous" comes in.

The beginning and end of each word can be identified by designated start and stop bits. Now, as long as both ends of the system (the computer and the external device) can agree on the baud rate (usually determined by the setting of the I/O board), the start and stop bits that are added to the digital word can tell the computer when a word starts and when it ends. There can be any length of time between words as long as the start and stop bits are added to do the "handshaking."

The 110-baud rate mentioned for the Teletype is that machine's standard speed both for the keyboard and tape reader. It means that 100 words per minute are being transmitted. This is the industry standard for slow-speed data exchange. This code takes 100 milliseconds to send one character. The 300-baud rate (generally used by CRT terminals and the hobbyist's tape system) means that 300 words per minute can be transmitted. Although at first this may seem fast, keep in mind that a typical computer can operate up to 25,000 baud!

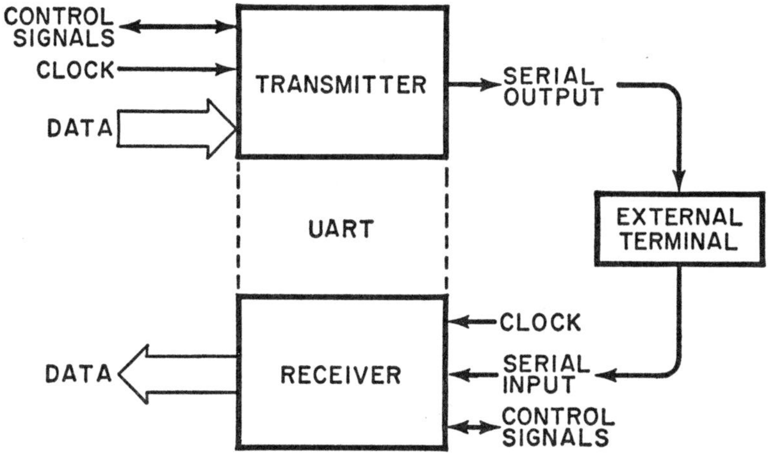

Figure 11.1 A UART contains a logic receiver and a logic transmitter. It allows communication with the outside world.

Now, let us take a look at the operation of a UART (see Figure 11.1). Although our discussion relates to the UART, some manufacturers are supplying other UART-like devices that do the same thing but under software control.

A UART needs a clock — something to keep all the data bits in step. Because of circuit considerations, a UART requires a clock frequency that is 16 times the selected baud rate; for example, a 110-baud rate circuit must have a clock with a frequency of 1760 Hz. For the 300-baud rate the clock must operate at 4800 Hz. Most I/O boards have some form of "strapping" to set the baud rate (actually they are setting up the clock frequency to the correct speed). Baud-rate strapping is usually explained in the manual for the I/O board.

In the UART transmitter section the computer "fills" a buffer with the required number of bits and after a "handshake" signal (which occurs when the buffer is filled) allows the data to exit one bit at a time. Each data bit must be in step with a clock pulse. In the UART "receive mode" the outside device fills the buffer, and when the buffer is full a handshake dumps the complete digital word into the computer in parallel form.

Now let us follow the UART-transmitted signal which has assumed serial form and see how it gets to the TTY or CRT terminal.

Before this can be done we must have some understanding of how a Teletype works. A TTY contains two sections: a transmitter consisting of the keyboard and any associated tape reader and the receiver consisting of the printer and any associated tape perforator. Although they are two separate sections, they are mounted in the same housing and appear to be one piece. They are not electrically connected unless the machine is in "local" mode (via a front-panel switch) when the keyboard signals are passed directly to the printer. In local mode the machine communicates only with its printer, not with the outside world.

The other front-panel switch position is called "line" and it allows the two halves of the TTY to communicate with the outside signal source. Four wire leads are required; two for the printer and two for the keyboard.

The keyboard (transmitter) section of the TTY uses special electromechanical circuits that convert each keystroke into the pertinent ASCII code character. What is ASCII? The name ASCII stands for American Standard Code for Information Interchange and, as shown in Appendix C, consists of various combinations of ls and 0s to form all alphanumeric characters, plus a wide variety of control characters. ASCII is a special language that computers and I/O devices use to communicate with one another.

Looking at Figure 11.2, let us see how data are passed back and forth between the computer and the TTY. When the computer sends data to the TTY, it makes and breaks a special 20-mA current circuit (usually on the I/O board). This current circuit drives special electromechanical devices in the TTY serial-to-parallel converter. Once a complete "word" is accumulated, the mechanism causes the pertinent TTY key to strike the paper and make its mark. This flow is dc and therefore has a positive and negative lead. The TTY input connectors are ap-

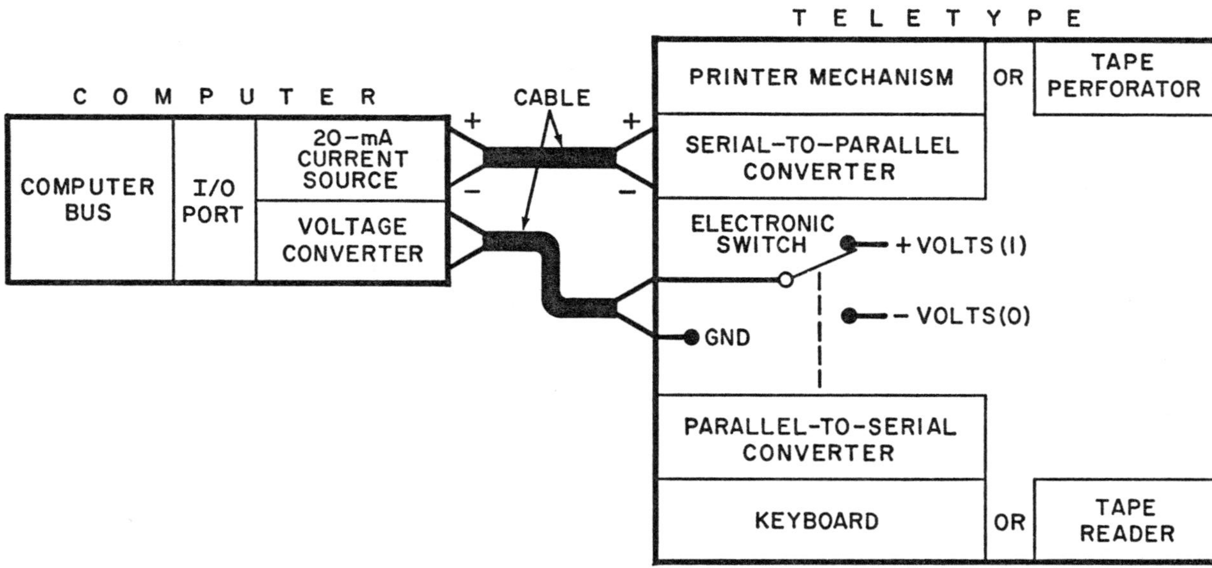

Figure 11.2 How data passes between a computer and a Teletype.

propriately marked so that the correct connections can be made. If the leads are reversed, the TTY will not print. In some Teletypes a tape perforator (a mechanical punch that makes hole patterns in paper tape 1/2 inch wide) can be used instead of the printing mechanism. This system is employed when a program is to be saved on paper tape.

When a key on the keyboard is activated, it operates an electromechanical system that makes and breaks a switch with the ASCII code for the letter on the key. In the input section of the I/O port a dual-polarity voltage source is keyed by the switch closings from the TTY. A positive voltage at the port causes a 1 to be entered and a negative voltage produces a 0. Because the TTY in this case merely opens and closes a switch, this portion of the TTY is not polarity-sensitive and the two leads for this section can be connected in either way on the two input connectors.

Therefore a Teletype requires two kinds of signal source: a current source for the printer mechanism and a voltage source for the keyboard output.

The video terminal on the other hand uses the same voltage scheme (positive for 1 and negative for 0 for both sections—keyboard and CRT readout). This system is usually referred to as the RS-232.

There are other device communication standards, but at this time the hobbyist is concerned only with the 20-mA current loop and the RS-232 standards.

PARALLEL I/O PORTS

Parallel I/O ports is a new term which means that the computer data-bus 8-bits (byte), plus the handshake signal, are all available at the same time; then why not dump all the pertinent data at once? Special circuits called, interestingly enough, parallel ports, can be connected to the computer if high-speed data I/O is desired. By using this approach it is possible to insert, say, 8K BASIC into a computer in a matter of seconds rather than in the 10 to 20 minutes needed by the slower 110-baud TTY approach. One simple example of a useful parallel-port entry device is the Oliver tape reader which is available at most computer stores. This is explained later in the chapter.

MASS STORAGE — CASSETTE

Up to this time we have talked about printing data on a TTY or displaying the data on a CRT screen. Now, what can you do if you want to save a program or some data? Of course, you can always perforate a paper tape by using the TTY, but such TTYs are expensive and the process is slow. You can always observe the data on the CRT and write it down on a piece of paper and then painfully type it into the computer whenever you need it. If you have lots of money, you can use a floppy disk (more on this later), but that method is expensive also. There must be an easier way!

The easy approach is called cassette recording which uses a conventional low-cost, audio-cassette/tape recorder/and a low-cost cassette. But, wait a moment, you may say—a digital computer operates with discrete digital ls and 0s and a tape recorder operates with speech or music. How is this done?

Suppose we have selected two different audio tones, both within the recording range of the cassette, and use one tone for 1 and the other for 0? In this way we can use the low-cost cassette recorder and its cassettes.

Although there are many different tone standards, and just about every computer manufacturer has his favorite, some use what is called the "Kansas City standard," which was set up by a group of hobby-computer manufacturers back in 1975. The Kansas City standard uses 2400-Hz for 1 and 1200-Hz for 0.

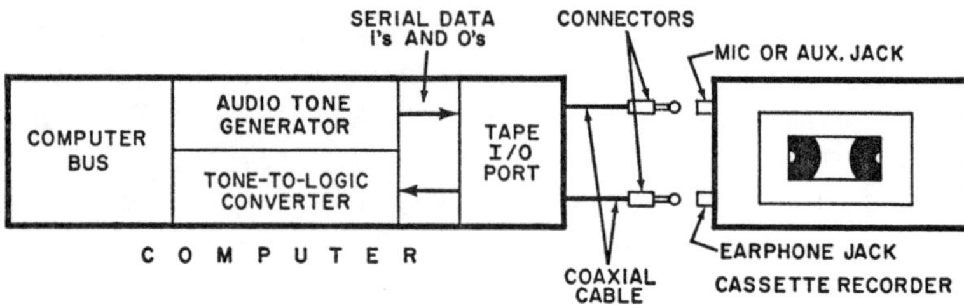

Figure 11.3 Communication between a computer and a cassette recorder.

During the last year or two many peripheral manufacturers introduced variations of interface boards for cassette recording, but most of them operate in the same way.

As shown in Figure 11.3, a special audio oscillator, operating at 2400-Hz in conjunction with a "divide-by-2" IC chip, is keyed by the computer to produce the correct string of 1s and 0s that forms the data. This string of serial tones is then plugged into the cassette recorder's microphone or auxiliary input jack and recorded on the cassette tape. During playback the audio tones are picked off the cassette tape, amplified by the tape recorder system, and fed via the earphone connector to the tape recorder input connector on the cassette interface board. The recording and playback speed of this tone system can be almost anything that the user chooses, which is one of the troubles with the whole idea. There are so many different audio-cassette recording systems on the market that a hobbyist is hard put to make up his mind about the one to use. When planning to buy or build, the speed of recording and playback should not be the major consideration. The user should find out which system has the greatest software support among the people with whom he is likely to exchange programs. In fact, he may have a 300-baud tape interface with which to interchange tapes and another that operates at a much faster speed for use with his own computer and tape player. The slow-speed 300-baud system permits tape interchange over telephone lines by using modems (telephone couplers) and also allows for variations in the speed of low-cost players. If you are going to use your tape recorder only to record data and play them back to your own computer, you can select any speed that works for you.

MODEMS

Although not used by many hobbyists, the modem (acronym for *mo*dulator-*dem*odulator) permits one computer to "talk" to another or one terminal to pass data to a computer or to another terminal via conventional telephone lines or other limited bandwidth communication channels. If you intend to do any time sharing (i.e., in which several terminals are connected to one computer via phone lines), the modem is the only way to go. All you need to do in most cases is dial the telephone number of the computer and, when it "answers," insert your telephone handset into the acoustic coupler of the modem, as shown in Figure 11.4. Once this is done you can start using your terminal as if it were directly connected to the computer. In this way a single computer can be made to service a number of "subscribers," and although a large number of terminals can be using the computer at the same time the computer may be switching around between terminals so fast that each operator will think he is the only one on the line.

As shown in Figure 11.4, modems use a tone system similar to that employed by cassette tape recorders. Modems can operate in one direction only — called half-duplex — or in both directions at the same time — called full duplex. Although most modems can operate at 9600 baud, full duplex operation over an ordinary telephone (bandwidth-limited) usually limits the speed to about 300 baud. Many modems employ two different sets of audio

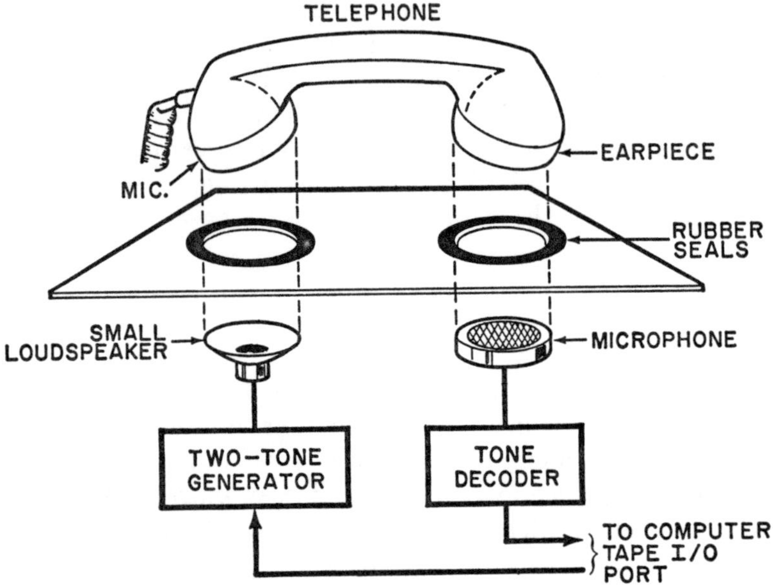

Figure 11.4 A modem or acoustic coupler. In this case an ordinary telephone line links two computers.

tones called high/low bands: one for transmitting and the other for receiving.

Physically, a modem looks like a small rectangular box with two large holes in its upper surface spaced for the telephone handset microphone and earpiece. Each hole is surrounded by a soft rubber seal to form a tight fitting around earpiece and microphone to block out extraneous noises. Some modems have front-panel switches that allow half-or full duplex operation and tape recording of data.

Actually there are two ways to get a telephone line into a modem. One is a direct-wire connection which uses a coupler supplied by the telephone compnay. Most hobbyists, however, go the acoustic coupling route shown in Figure 11.4, which means that no direct connections are made to the phone line. A small speaker talks into the phone microphone while a small microphone listens at the earphone end.

FLOPPY DISK

This relatively expensive approach to mass storage combines tape recording and audio record techniques. The disk is a large piece of magnetic recording medium cut into the shape of a record. It revolves on a center spindle just as a record does, but the recording/pickup head does not move in a spiral fashion. Instead the magnetic head moves across the disk in a straight line and the tracks on the disk are not connected. The disk controller electronics cause the head to move to any particular track to record or pick up data. Typical disks can store many hundreds of thousands of digital words and some can store millions.

There are two types of disk — hard and floppy. A hard disk is stiff and somewhat like a conventional plastic phonograph record. The floppy disk is made of thinner material and "floppy." Both types of disk usually come in protective packaging and the raw disk is never exposed to human contact (finger oils). Recording and playback are usually made through a small window in the protective shield.

OTHER I/O DEVICES

Until recently the only way to "read" paper tapes into a computer was to use a relatively expensive ASR-33 Teletype equipped with a tape reader (also a tape perforator). To read a paper tape the tape is inserted into a special tape guide and a plastic tape retainer is clamped over it. When the TTY switch is placed in the tape read position, a sprocket wheel pulls the tape over a set of seven slender metal fingers that come up under it. If there is a hole in the tape immediately above any of the fingers, the finger passes through the tape. In doing so the bottom of the metal finger makes contact with an electric bar in the tape reader to complete an electric circuit similar to that of a keyboard key being depressed. The ASCII combination of the contacting fingers then forms the word to be transmitted or typed on the TTY.

This means that the relatively weak paper tape has to withstand the repeated impacts of the metal fingers probing for their holes; unfortunately this action often tears it at its weak points. Thus erratic data can be introduced into the progam played back by the tape. The action of the sprocket wheel that pulls the paper tape along can damage it also.

Another problem introduced by the tape reader, already discussed, is speed. For the most of us the 110-baud of the TTY is too slow. It can take as long as 15 minutes to enter a typical 8K BASIC. If you have a longer program, more time will be needed.

Some commercial tape readers can operate at very fast speeds, but they are expensive, and unless you happen to find one at a low price at a flea market you won't see many of them around.

The commercial tape readers that operate at high speeds use the optical reader system in which a light is concentrated on a narrow section of the moving tape. A set of light-sensitive cells is arranged in a row across the width of the tape and as the tape moves the light shines through the holes into the light cells, but not through the unbroken paper. There are eight sensors for data and one for the sprocket hole. Most of these optical tape readers are expensive, but Oliver Audio Engineering, a West Coast firm, has introduced a low-cost unit that is sold in most computer stores.

To use this tape reader the user threads the paper tape through tape guides at the top of the reader and adjusts a light source to shine down on the tape-sensor combination. The tape is then pulled manually through the guides as fast as the user desires. This is a parallel-port device that will operate as fast as your computer will accept the data. By using this device 8K

BASIC can be loaded in a matter of seconds and there is no wear on the tape unless you tear it by pulling too fast.

VIDEO DISPLAYS

General

Video displays are the TV-like devices that you see working with computers and displaying data on a CRT screen. There are several types: first, the video terminal, which is a self-contained unit equipped with a keyboard, video character generator, and CRT display. The video terminal is connected directly to the computer or by a modem via telephone lines to a remote machine. They are the video equivalent of a TTY or other printer terminal. Some low-cost video terminals are suitable for use with a personal computer. Southwest Technical Products makes the CT-64 Video Terminal Kit for $325, Micro-Term, Inc. makes the Act-1, a complete terminal less the CRT, for only $400, and Micon Industries makes the "Captain Video" series. Several of the manufacturers of commercial video terminals now offer kit versions of their regular units. The Lear Siegler ADM-3A kit and the SOROC Technology IQ 120 kit are examples. When assembled, they are equal to the commercial versions. Their cost is less than $1000 in kit form, a price that is low by industry standards but high for a hobbyist.

The answer to this problem has been the development of video display modules that convert the digital output of the data bus into alphanumeric video signals. These modules are boards that plug directly into the computer bus and output video signals to an external video monitor or converted TV set.

Video Monitors

There are two types of video monitor: those specifically designed to work with a computer or video-generating device and a converted TV set. The regular video monitor works much better because it is designed specifically for this purpose and will clearly display the full 80-character output of a video terminal. The converted TV set will not display 80 characters clearly because it was not designed for this application. It will work well with 64 characters per line; thus most video displays designed for hobbyists generate this maximum of 64.

Some hobbyists neither wish to buy a video monitor nor convert a black and white TV and therefore attempt to use an RF converter and an unmodified TV set. Several versions of one or two transistor TV transmitters or converters are available. They accept the composite video signals from the video display module in the computer and convert them into an RF signal that will pass from the set's antenna terminals through the TV front end into the video circuits. Several things are wrong with this idea. First, most of these kits are not type-approved by the FCC and are therefore illegal. Second, aside from graphics displays, they don't work very well. If you want to convert a TV set into a monitor, use a black and white set with an isolation power transformer and perform the conversion according to instructions in one of the magazines or in Don Lancaster's excellent *TVT Cookbook,* published by Howard W. Sams and on sale at your local computer store.

Several TV manufacturers will soon be offering models with video input connections and switches to disconnect the antennas. They are doing this for the TV game market and their own video tape recorders, but the computer hobbyist will benefit.

Video Display Modules

The first video display module suitable for use by the hobbyist was the VDM-1 produced by the Processor Technology Corporation. This unit plugs into the S-100 bus and generates 16 lines of 64 characters across the screen. It can produce white characters on a black background or black characters on a white background. In addition, it scrolls like an expensive video terminal and is very fast, for it can fill the screen with data in an instant. It has its own memory and the user can control the writing speed on the screen. The VDM-1 also has limited graphics capability and is considered as the standard with which other video displays are compared. Similar boards are made by other manufacturers and advertised in hobby publications.

PolyMorphic Systems makes a video display for its Poly-88 that is also used in other S-100 bus systems. This unit has a parallel input port suitable for the connection of a keyboard. The Poly video module can therefore be the only I/O board in a video output computer.

A new entry on the video display market is the Merlin, two boards that plug into the Altair/S-100 bus and generate both alphanumeric characters and complex graphic patterns. The Merlin also has PROMs that contain data monitor software and can be programmed to produce any kind of character desired.

Other computer manufacturers have provided their machines with video capabilities. The entire Digital Group concept features video output and their video displays, often used in hobbyist "home brew" systems, are excellent.

OSI, Apple Computer, MicroMind, Wave Mate, and Sphere also use video-module-based systems of high quality. Because the cost of "hard copy" terminals exceeds the cost of most personal computers, it seems that video display provides the most cost effective way to present data.

The TV Dazzler

Cromemco Inc. has produced one of the most unusual video displays ever invented. It is called the TV Dazzler and it plugs into the Altair/S-100 bus. Using programs provided by Cromemco or developed by the operator, the Dazzler provides fantastic displays of full color graphics on a color TV receiver or monitor. It can be programmed to produce alphanumerics or color patterns and introduces the element of creative art into the home computer field. Cromemco also produces an analog-to-digital and digital-to-analog converter board called the D-7A, which can be connected to "joystick" controls, also supplied by Cromemco, and installed in the computer to control the color patterns on the Dazzler in real-time applications. The hobbyist can use one of the approved RF converters with his color TV to eliminate the difficult job of converting a color set.

TV Display

Most computers can be provided with a built-in or plug-in video display module to convert computer data to alphanumerics for display on a TV-like screen.

There are four ways in which this visual display can be accomplished:

The first is to have the computer's video system built within the computer enclosure. This is done in most commercial and a couple of the newer hobby systems. Obviously the cost of the video display is added to the cost of the computer system.

In the second approach, which is the most common and the easiest to implement, the computer video display is terminated with a video coaxial cable that can be plugged directly into a commercial video monitor. Video monitors come in all screen sizes and can be purchased at any computer hobby store.

The third approach uses an FCC (Federal Communications Commission) approved RF (radio frequency) modulator whose input accepts the video cable from the computer and whose output can be tuned to a locally unused low-band (2 through 6) TV channel. These small RF modulators must be approved by the FCC because they transmit RF that can interfere with commercial broadcasting. Use of such a modulator means that any TV receiver can act as a video monitor simply by connecting the modulator output directly to the TV receiver antenna terminals and tuning them both to an unused channel. Because of certain electronic problems (primarily bandwidth problems), do not expect a sharp and crisp image. For most hobby uses, however, this type of display works well and is the lowest priced approach to video display.

The fourth approach is not recommended for the beginner. It involves rebuilding a conventional TV receiver so that it uses only its internal video amplifiers and sweep sections. The selected TV receiver must have power-line isolation in the interests of safety and special video connectors have to be added. This conversion must be done by a qualified TV technician, for there is considerable danger of shock and possible electrocution in addition to severe damage to the computing system if the conversion is not correctly made.

12 Software

When all test programs have been completed, and your computer is up and running, it will just blink its lights at you, waiting for software.

WHAT IS SOFTWARE AND WHERE DO YOU GET IT?

In computerese, software constitutes the programs that operate a computer and instructions in their use. Everybody has heard of computer programs, but let us consider exactly what they are. Although the preceding chapters have described the operation of the computers and their number systems, we repeat some of the information for clarity.

A computer consists of a group of registers or places to store numbers. The numbers can be information (called data) or instructions to the computer. Programming merely causes data to move from one register to another and to perform the operations of addition, subtraction, multiplication, and division, according to the set of instructions. A programmer must learn to manipu-

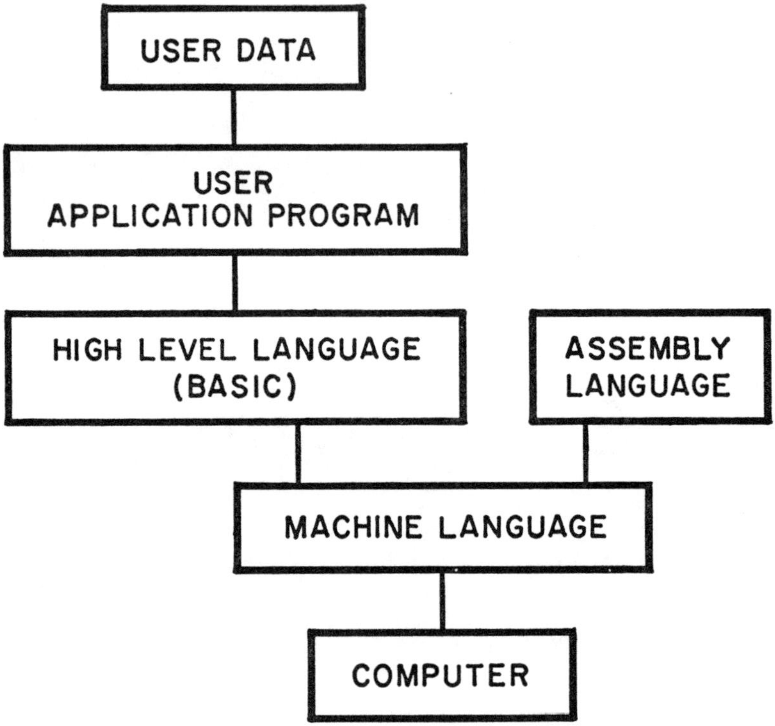

Figure 12.1 The heirarchy of languages.

late the instructions to make meaningful transfers from one register to another and the correct arithmetic operations. The most important thing the programmer must learn, however, is the translation of ordinary language into unambiguous computer instructions. Some common instructions are used by all computers, but each microprocessor has its unique set. The scope and variety of these instructions determine its power (Figure 12.1).

MACHINE LANGUAGE

The instruction set of the microprocessor is called machine language. You don't have to go out to find it because it is there inside the microprocessor. You do have to learn at least the common instructions to understand your microcomputer. Computers usually come with a manual that explains the machine language of the microprocessor. Instructions are grouped according to the type of work they do and the method of entering them. In some more than 1 byte is used to give the instruction and the memory address from which the instruction is to be obtained or in which it is to be placed.

The computer must be told in machine language to perform each step of an operation; for example, in order to add two numbers the computer must know where to get the numbers (from keyboard input port), where to store them (in an accumulator), what to do with them (add), where to store the result (in an accumulator or memory location), and, if desired, where to output the result (output port).

Because this type of detailed operation must be done for everything that the computer does, you may ask, "Why use machine language at all?" The answer is that machine language is the only one in which the computer knows how to work. Higher level languages in which you ask the computer 2 + 2 = and it answers 4 are general programs that run in machine language. Their use imposes an overhead burden on the computer in terms of memory and speed. If you are entering data in an accounting program written in Extended BASIC, what you are really doing is running a program, written within a program, that is itself written in machine language. If the accounting program were written directly in machine language, it would allow more space in memory and run faster and more efficiently. It would also not be easily convertible from one computer to another.

Because of this characteristic, machine-language programs designed to accomplish specific tasks are desirable and are sold as products for each computer by software designers. The vendor usually installs the program on the machine and makes the modifications necessary to run it with the computer configuration.

Users are willing to pay for these programs in spite of the fact that similar ones are written in high-level languages and are in the public domain because their cost is small in view of the saving in time and memory. For the hobbyist this may not hold true because the cost of memory is low and time is not money. The size of the hobby computer, however, is fixed and not easily expandable, and even the hobbyist must make the decision on what level language to operate.

ASSEMBLY LANGUAGE

Because the computer understands only the 1s and 0s of binary arithmetic and it is hard to use them, monitor programs that permit the machine code to be entered in hex or octal form are provided.

Some computers contain several hundred instructions and most people find it hard to remember them all. The computer itself, however, can quite easily remember all the codes for the instructions. Therefore programs called assemblers are written to do it for you. For each computer instruction there is an abbreviation called a mnemonic, which is a combination of letters, such as LDA for load accumulator A, that is easy to remember. The assembly language also does other things such as figuring where to jump to on jump instructions (a subject that is beyond the scope of this discussion). The user of an assembler enters the program in the form of mnemonics, edits the typing errors, and then tells the computer to assemble the program at a certain starting point in memory. The result, if printed out on a terminal, is a block of machine code with which the computer can run the program.

The program can be stored in two ways:

1. The computer can output to magnetic tape, disk, or punched paper tape the ASCII (see Appendix) code for the mnemon-

ics used in the program. Because there is a seven-digit binary code for each letter, the tape is reproducible on any terminal that uses this code system. This is called a source tape and when printed out produces a source listing which anyone who knows the mnemonics used in the assembly language can understand.

2. The other type of output is a tape or disk of the assembled machine code for the program. This is called the object tape and can be used only to run the program on an identical type of computer. It must be noted that if there is to be any program change the entire program must be reassembled and a new object tape made. An experienced user, however, can make changes or "patches" in the program by going to the correct memory location and changing the machine language code. He must remember to make a new object tape or the next time the program is loaded it will be unchanged.

HIGH-LEVEL LANGUAGES

From the preceding discussions it can be seen why the programming of computers became such a deep mystery after their invention. The practice of programming became the business of a group of specialists. To make the computer useful to the people who needed it, without the help of middlemen, simplified ways of writing programs had to be found. The result is a large group of languages that removes the drudgery of standard operations and permits the user to instruct the computer in simpler terms. These languages have many names, most of which people today have heard: FORTRAN, COBOL, ALGOL, BASIC, and APL, to name a few. In all cases the high-level language simulates with the computer the methods people use to solve problems in mathematics, business, and science. Once a user can operate in familiar terms and methods he needs no one between him and the computer.

High-level languages are of two general classifications: first came the compiler type in which, typically, the user wrote a program in FORTRAN or COBOL. The program was punched on a deck of cards and fed into the computer. The computer assembled the program and produced an object code deck of cards, or tape, which could then be used. If anything was wrong with the program, the computer would not run it and the writer would have to redo it and have it completely reassembled (or compiled).

With the development of time sharing and minicomputers in which the user is in direct command of the computer a new group of languages was developed called interpreters because they made the computer stop and assemble each line of a program as it was entered from a keyboard. If an error was made, it could be corrected at once. In fact, most high-level languages will return an error message at the end of a line when an error is made and the computer does not understand the entry. Most hobby computer high-level languages use these interpreters. They are much slower than the compiled languages and this may be important in large programs. Today there are interactive compiled languages in which the user enters the program from a keyboard directly into the computer (or reads a tape or disk). The program is immediately compiled and the machine code is run or recorded.

In some cases the mechanics of the operation are transparent to the user, who does not know whether the program is an interpreter or a compiler. Most hobby or personal computers can be used with either type of high-level language, but until now few compiled high-level languages have been developed for microcomputers. Any number of cross-assembled programs are used with microcomputers in which the source program is entered and run on a large computer. The result is an object tape or disk which can be run on the microcomputer. This is not a satisfactory method for personal computing because of its complexity.

APPLICATION PROGRAMS

Application programs are the payoff in computing, for they are the means by which real work is done. Regardless of the use of the program, the method by which the computer does real calculating and storage is called an application program. Obtaining application programs becomes the principal activity after a computer is built and running.

As a start, the various magazines are a source of usable programs and instructions on how to write your own. Learning a high-level language and the machine language of the computer increases the pleasure of owning one. For most the construction of a computer is only a means to an end. The end is writing and using useful programs.

Another source of application programs is found in the clubs. People who write interesting programs often want to share them. Sometimes they sell them to finance their hobby and sometimes they put them in the club library for free use. In any event, a hobbyist will find great pleasure in being able to think out a problem, draw a flowchart of the proposed solution, and then implement it with a program that works. Books are another source of application programs, but many of them seem to cost a great deal more than ordinary volumes. This is an attempt by the writers to recover the large expense of software development from a relatively small market. You are not only paying for a book but for usable software.

FIRMWARE

A new method of program distribution is provided by the use of Read Only Memory. Programs can be burned into PROMs and installed in computers for immediate availability when the machine is turned on. This is a step toward producing a utility computer that anyone can use. At this time, however, mostly bootstrap and monitor programs are being provided in PROMs. A few computers have the entire high-level language in PROM, but most provide it in the form of a tape or disk. As volume production and improved technology force the cost of PROMs down, though, more and more software will be provided as firmware modules. The result will be a computer dedicated to business problems with all the programs in the computer for use by people with no knowledge of the machine operation. Modules that the hobbyist can plug into his computer and produce his own firmware give him more time to enjoy its use and free him from the chores of loading programs used to bootstrap other programs in and out of his machine. These new modules employ a form of PROM that is erasable by ultraviolet light or electric current. They are called EPROMs (Erasable Programmable Read Only Memory) and are read only—write sometimes memory. As costs come down these chips will promote the exchange of software and information among users and will encourage the sale of programs in a simple usable form.

SOFTWARE-IN-A-MAGAZINE

Because there is no easy way of distributing programs to the personal computer user in a uniform format, several of the magazines in the field have advanced new ideas on methods of distribution. *BYTE* has suggested that programs be printed in magazines in bar code. This is a simple method of printing lines with various spaces in a vertical column. The pick-up is an optical reader or "wand" which reflects a beam of light onto the bar code and scans the reflected light and dark areas as it is moved down the column of bars. This coding and reading is now appearing on food packages and other supermarket items. There is no reason why magazines could not use the same method to publish software. As more and more programs become available in bar code, wands and bar code interfaces will be on sale in the stores. Some of the implications of this idea have not yet been explored, but it may also permit us to store huge amounts of software in inexpensive, permanent form.

Interface Age has another method of distributing programs to its readers. Taking note that most hobbyists have audio-cassette interfaces for use with their computers, *Interface Age* is binding "floppy records" into copies of their publication. These are thin plastic records designed to be played back on a home phonograph. The audio output is connected from the output jack on the audio amplifier to the cassette input cable for the cassette interface. After the program is loaded into the computer correctly it is recorded on the regular cassette for future use. The record is retained only as a backup because this type of record cannot be used too often.

13 What Can You Do with a Computer?

This question is probably the one that most nonhobbyists ask computer enthusiasts. The reply can become difficult once you get past the game-playing and number-crunching answers.

Although the science-fiction image of a complete computer-controlled environment is still in the future, even at this time it is possible to build or buy output ports that will allow almost any computer to accept data from a great variety of sensors and produce control signals that will energize almost any electric appliance.

ELECTRIC POWER CONTROL

One example of a controller board is the MITS 88-PCI, which can work with the Altair 8800 or 680. This board contains the equivalent of eight single-pole-single-throw relays which can control up to 1 ampere at 120 volts ac. It can be used to control motors, fans, contactors, alarms, solenoids, lights, heaters, and just about any other electric appliance. It also has eight input terminals that can be configured by the user to accept almost any kind of data, operate on them, and use the result to control some electric peripheral.

Around the house, for example, a small computer equipped with a controller I/O system can be used to operate a lawn sprinkler, turn lights on and off at predetermined intervals, or even act as a combination alarm clock and "cook," for it will also power up a coffee pot or electric frying pan before the user gets to the kitchen (just remember those frosty mornings).

Obviously electric power control will find many applications in business, around a farm or factory, and just about anywhere electric appliances are being used. In ham radio, for example, this system can direct a beam antenna for maximum signal strength, keep logbooks, or send automatic CQs while the operator listens out. If you are a photography bug, this system can keep tabs on the various chemical processes in the dark room. Thermistors can watch over liquid temperatures and turn on heaters when the temperature drops below some predetermined level. On the farm the system can watch over liquid flowmeters and keep pumps operating. You can make automatic weighing installations, control hoppers, and thereby material flow, and set temperatures in different areas according to need. The tasks that a control system can perform are uncounted, and once this area has been investigated many new uses will come along.

All you have to do is determine what you want monitored and the type of sensor that will be needed. You will then require an interface between that sensor and the computer input. Next you determine what you want the computer to do about the "problem" and connect the output port to some electric device that will achieve it. The last step is a program to control the whole operation. None of the above is difficult if you look at what is available at your local computer store and talk to the people at your computer club. The hardest part is getting started.

REMOTE CONTROL BY COMPUTER

In order to control remote electric appliances, some means must be found to allow the computer to "talk" to the applicable power socket. This is the stone wall that most computer hobbyists run into when they want their computers to "do" things around the house, apartment, or farm, and this is where they sometimes come to a grinding stop. It is not an insurmountable problem, however. One solution is to employ the technique commonly used by a wireless intercom on which one can communicate with other rooms or offices.

In a wireless intercom/the voice input modulates a high-frequency oscillator (usually several hundred kHz) and the modulated output signal is applied to the power line. The wireless receiver input is also connected to the ac line (isolated for safety) and the receiver portion is tuned to the same frequency as the remote transmitter. The receiver than demodulates the voice signal, amplifies it, and applies it to a loudspeaker so that it can be heard. This is like any other two-way radio frequency system, except that the frequencies are only a couple of hundred kilohertz (kHz), and the means of "transmitting" the signal are the conventional power lines.

Figure 13.1 shows how the idea can be adapted to the use of a computer to control devices. The necessary wireless intercom units can be purchased from almost any electronics supply house.

The wireless transmitter is fed from a tone generator and the frequency of each tone is determined by the computer output signal. The computer-selected tone then modulates the transmitter and the forthcoming signal is applied to the power line, which allows it to be received anywhere on the premises.

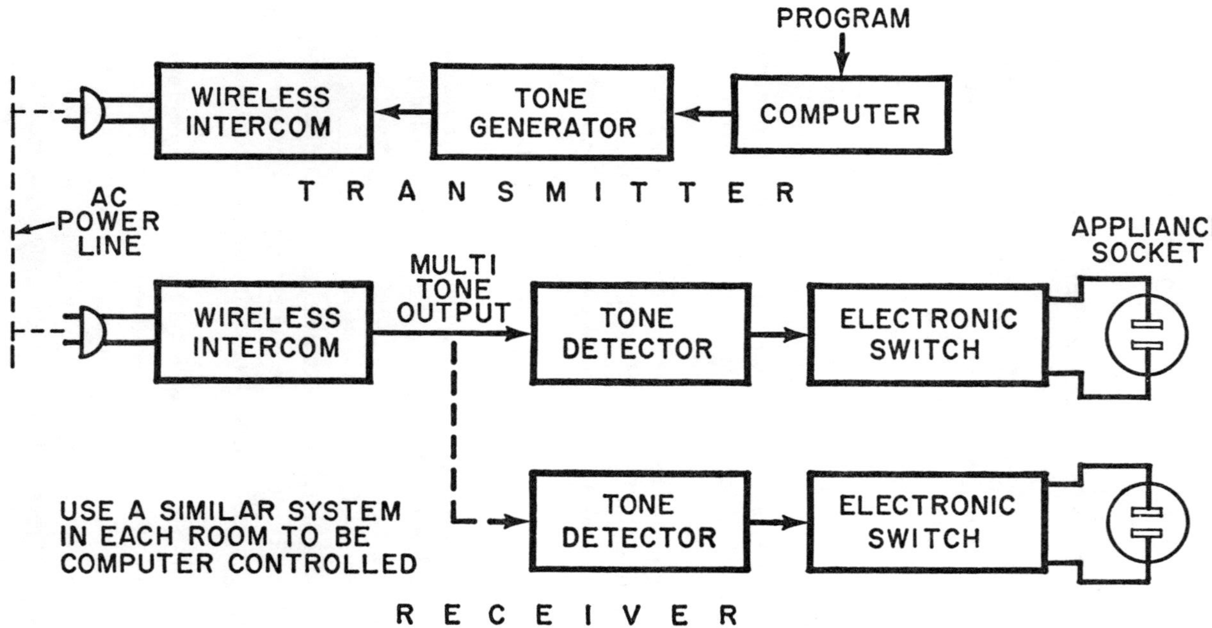

Figure 13.1 Remote control by computer. In this arrangement the computer controls a device by using house wiring that already exists.

Each room that contains controlled appliances will have a signal control box equipped with a carrier-current receiver to demodulate the audio tones. The audio output "bus" is applied to a number of tone detectors which in turn, control the power applied to its associated power socket. You can have almost any number of controlled sockets in each remote control box, but make sure that each is clearly identified either by number or color.

When a tone decoder receives the tone frequency to which it has been tuned, it activates an SCR or Triac to apply power to its socket. Although no construction details are given, and imaginative reader can see that a low-cost wireless intercom, a handful of tone-decoder ICs (phase-locked loops), and some power Triacs or SCRs are all that is required. A conventional flip-flop can be connected between each tone decoder output and the associated Triac or SCR so that a time signal need be transmitted only once for socket turn on and again for socket turn off.

GAMES

Guessing games have probably been around since man first learned to communicate with his fellows. Various forms of checkers and chess probably go back a thousand years or so, and each generation seems to "reinvent" many of the old forms. Myriad versions of two-or-more-person games, including all the card games and their variations, have sprung up since the first deck of cards made its appearance.

Now a new element has entered the scene—the digital computer. Not having any intelligence at all but merely able to "understand" and play by the rules, a digital computer can be programmed to create a formidable opponent in just about any game that two people can play, and because a computer can make many thousands of decisions in a fraction of a second it can compete with and, in most cases, beat its human opponent.

During the last several years, long before there were any hobby computers, programmers created a great number of man-machine "interactive" games such as poker, checkers, Go, and Tic-Tac-Toe and various mathematical games such as Nim and magic squares—far too many to list here. Most of these games can be found in "computer game" books at your local computer store. You may be surprised at the complexity of some of them.

Trek

One of the most famous and popular games is "Star Trek," which is based on the popular TV series. Many of its variations are complex and require large amounts of memory to implement. Some are simple and are used as "trainers," others need graphics for display, but almost all follow the same script.

Programs usually start by telling the user how many Klingons (bad guys) are out there in deep space and that you (the computer operator) have one starship (the *Enterprise*) with which to hunt down and eliminate them from the deep voids. Your space cruiser is equipped with all sorts of weapons like phasors and photon torpedoes, but some games give you other esoteric tools such as laser lances, antimatter bombs, and other highly destructive "goodies."

Your space cruiser has "deflector screens" that can absorb a certain number of hits from the nasty Klingons, but each time you are "hit" your available energy is reduced. If it gets too low, you have to look around for a "starbase" where you can refuel and take on another load of weapons. The game starts by positioning the *Enterprise* in some quadrant of space that can be seen on the "short-range sensors." Stars, starbases, Klingons, and unknowns all have their own particular symbols, and after a brief run you will learn to recognize what is near you in that quadrant.

The "long-range sensor scan" allows you to see the quadrants that immediately surround yours, and this, as a rule, turns up as a series of three digits. The first is the number of Klingons in that quadrant, the second (middle) digit is the number of starbases, and the last is the number of stars. Two methods of flight are used—impulse, which allows you to move around the quadrant you are presently occupying, and warp, which allows you to jump between quadrants.

Most games will also give you a direct readout of the various energy levels, such as warp/impulse power, phasor power, torpedo-tube power, the number of torpedoes remaining and deflector screen power, and will tell you how much power remains in the spaceship; other combinations give you the present star date (you are allowed so many star dates to wipe out the Klingons) and the quadrant alert status (green for no Klingons and red when a Klingon is in the same quadrant as the *Enterprise*). The number of Klingons remaining is also supplied.

The game is played in two dimensions: you can "fly" up, down, and at almost any angle in between. These directions are spelled out in the instructions.

Once you have popped into a quadrant you must avoid hitting (flying into) a star, a Klingon, or an unknown (in some games strange things may happen if you "phasor," "torpedo," or ram into an unknown). You must take advantage of any weapon at your command, but always keep in mind that while the *Enterprise* is hunting the Klingon he is firing at you. In most games you cannot sit around trying to come up with a strategy; you have to get right to work or suffer the consequences. Some games introduce "triton mines" or other deadly space debris left around by unknown aliens. They can cause weird things to happen (or not happen) if you annoy one of them in any way!

You can lose command of your on-board computer and any orders you give may not come out right; this gets interesting when you are surrounded by unknowns or triton mines. You can even jump into "hyperspace," where all the laws of physics you know so well do not apply. Up is no longer up, but sideways, warp power may fire the photon torpedoes, and other dandy things.

If you are good (or lucky), in an hour or so you may be drifting around in space without a starbase in sight, waiting for your self-destruct sequence to start, or you may have wiped out the Klingons and been promoted to admiral. If things turn real bad, you may be transferred to an Earth-Moon garbage scow!

Unfortunately there aren't many starbases around where you can refuel and reload, so you have to keep a map of where things are—things like Klingons and starbases. Most versions of Star Trek are anything but easy, despite the fact that you have almost all the movements around the various quadrants. It is still a simple matter to get into serious trouble. Of course, if the worst comes, you can always reset the computer and start the game over, a little smarter this time.

Some variations of Star Trek are played between schools or computer clubs with one computer flying the *Enterprise,* another flying the Klingon battlecruiser or fleet, and possibly a third acting as referee. Some games have gone on for months.

Luna Lander

If space is your interest but you have no desire to dash around popping off Klingons, there are a number of variations of what are usually called lunar landers. In this computer game you are placed in orbit around the moon at some specified altitude. The object is to fire rocket thrusters that will permit you to touch down on the moon's surface with close to zero velocity. The computer is always solving the orbit problem (just like the real thing), and each time you "brake" the computer prints a readout of altitude downward velocity, fuel remaining, and so on. The intent is a soft landing, although it seldom materializes (unless you are lucky or a professional astronaut), and you wind up at zero velocity 100 feet up and no fuel left, run out of fuel 50 feet up while in a rapid descent, or impact the moon at some horrible velocity that will bury you far out of sight! The computer will print out all the hairy details of what has happened to you.

Chess, Checkers, and Card Games

If space flight is not your dish, take a look at the myriad variations of chess, checkers, and card games. Most of the "Monte Carlo" games have been programmed for hobby computers. Just think of playing blackjack against the machine when you have a million dollars in your pocket, spinning a roulette wheel to see how your luck is, or having a computer "laugh" at you when you draw to an inside straight at poker and don't make it!

Children's Games

What about children? They have not been forgotten, and many interactive games are aimed right at the young ones—starting when they have just learned to read, right up to high school. One example of a beginners' learning game is Hurkle. Here the child tries to locate an invisible hurkle that is hiding somewhere on the monitor CRT screen by typing in what he or she thinks is the correct location. The computer answers (on screen) by telling the child how far away and in which direction the hurkle can be found. This is an easy way to teach children directions and graphs and how to visualize a situation. Computer games are probably one of the best teaching aids around, and because the computer has infinite patience it can repeat the training time after time without getting the least bit excited (as some parents seem to do).

In the many random-number guessing games, animal chases, and forms of "Jotto," sometimes bilingual, children must learn how to use words. In the bilingual games the question is asked in one language and the child answers in the other. In animal games the child must answer questions that the computer asks in order that the computer may identify the animal on which the child is concentrating.

All children's games are mind-stimulating and require exercise of the imagination and stimulation of visualization. There are many good program books at your local computer store that cover such games. Drop in and browse around.

BUSINESS APPLICATIONS

Many purchasers of personal computers hope to use them for business purposes. The ultimate purpose of these computers may well be some form of business system, but today many of the applications that people want are just not possible with the average personal computer system, for it lacks the ability to store and access files and to form files of data that are separate from programs in BASIC. Low-cost floppy disks and the newest versions of BASIC being written for them will be able to isolate and store files of data needed for business records.

For those who have more modest requirements simple household accounts and checkbook-balancing programs are now available with audio-cassettes that come with most machines.

This is a bit cumbersome but it can be done. Programs for a lot of business applications are being published in book form and are in the public domain. They include accounts payable and receivable, inventory, mailing lists, and billing and receiving.

The programs listed in many available books may not exactly fit the business of the user, but anyone with a small knowledge of BASIC can modify them to produce the kind of output reports required. Because specialized application programming is an expensive form of service, the small business may well be willing to change his system to fit the program.

In most cases the minimum system configuration required to operate a small business system will include a computer with at least 24K of memory, a disk system, and a printer or video terminal with an additional hard-copy printer. A backup tape cassette interface is also a good idea.

Because most systems, unlike commercial computers, will not operate on a round-the-clock basis, it is necessary to enter operating programs and data on disks. The operating procedure starts the computer, loads the business system program, and then loads the last data disk from the preceding day's operation. If the business program is written in BASIC, another step may be necessary to load the BASIC program. Most disks, however, have the capacity to load the BASIC language, the operating system, and the application software; the user then inserts his data disk and loads that. All data to be worked on are now in memory and the update can be performed. If large amounts of data must be processed, several disks may be used, and the data update done in blocks. After the day's business is entered and the files are updated the new data are written on a new disk and the daily report is printed out on the printer. An additional operation will dump the day's data onto a cassette to provide a safe backup. In some cases a backup may be made on paper tape. This is a slow method, but paper tape provides a universal format that could be read by another computer in the event of a breakdown.

The whole question of computer breakdown is not usually talked about, but even the largest and most powerful computers do go down. If this happens to a small system, the user may lose one day's data; if there is no backup, the loss could be greater. It is well to consider these facts before trusting vital data to a computer. Another question to be settled before using a small business system based on a personal computer is who repairs the system when it goes down and how fast can the repair be made. There is no service available from the manufacturer and most of the small dealers in personal computers have not yet offered help. The small businessman or software developer had best be cautious about dealing with mail-order or distant dealers of equipment. A local full-service dealer with field service facilities should be the only source of equipment for business systems because anything less will fail to render the necessary help. It should be noted that no dealer in the personal computer business can offer the kind of field service provided for large computers by their manufacturers. The best that can be expected is a system of board exchanges to get the system running again. This may result in a repair turn-around time of at least one day or more. If the user feels that this is not satisfactory, he should not consider a low-cost personal computer system.

To sum up this discussion of business systems the following list of requirements will be necessary for any application:

1. A reliable, well-made computer that has been "burned-in."
2. A good disk with an operating system designed for the computer and its software.
3. A proved application program. If it is written in BASIC, the high-level language should permit saving data files.
4. Enough memory to hold the maximum requirements anticipated.
5. Provision for both disk and a secondary backup data dump.
6. A service contract with fast board exchange maintenance.
7. A good printer for reports and program printouts.
8. Software that is adjustable to changing business situations.

All of this may seem like a lot to ask of computers that were only toys a short time ago, but even babies grow up. These personal computers have the power to become the foundation of business computing for everyone; all they need is a little development time and an understanding public.

WORD PROCESSING

The ability to compose text on a typewriter, edit it, and then have it typed back at any time has been given the name *word processing*. The necessary equipment has been provided by a number of large companies such as IBM and Xerox. Because so many people are interested in word-processing functions, it has become one of the most popular personal computing applications.

In order to use a microcomputer for word processing, several elements must be supplied. First the computer must have a video or typewriter terminal input. The text is composed on the terminal, fed into the computer, and stored on a tape or disk. Second, the system must have a program that enables the computer to display, add, delete, or change any part of the text. It must also be able to shift blocks of text from one location to another. Some text-editing routines also have the ability to search out any word or phrase in a body of text and replace it with another. This is one of the most powerful features of a good word-processing system; it can be included in a personal computing system if it has enough memory. This brings us the next requirement—memory.

In an 8-bit computer such as the 8080 or 6800 the minimum amount of memory required to run an effective word-processing system is about 16K; however, for a really complete system twice that amount is needed. One other requirement is a mass data storage system. Cassette tape can be used because most word-processing requirements are sequential in nature, but a floppy disk is much better because it provides faster access to the information.

A lot of the available word-processing programs are written in BASIC and therefore require much more memory because the BASIC program and then the word-processing program must be loaded. The text is typed in last. The computer memory must be large enough to support the several levels required to use all these programs. A text program that runs in machine language is much more efficient and several are available for the 8080 and 6800 machines. One of the most popular personal computers, the Sol, has a text-editing program in PROM that comes with the computer. The Sol program is called SOLED and is selected as an option.

The difference between a computer running a text-editing program and a full word-processing system is in the printer. In order to use a system for practical applications, its output must conform to the appearance of normal typed copy. Several typewriter terminals are available, some of which are based on the IBM ball used in Selectric machines and produce excellent text. It should be noted that these machines operate with an IBM code that is different from the normal ASCII (American Standard for Information Interchange) code used by most personal computers. Before buying any of these machines be sure that you have some method of converting the code into machine-usable form.

Some of the other typewriters use the DAISY print wheel. They are much higher in price and have not been around long enough to have reached the rebuilt or used market. In short, the printing unit of a word-processing system can cost more than the rest of the system. If this discourages the user, he should remember that the system will work with a less elegant typewriter, such as a Teletype. The text will then undergo only one retyping instead of the several required during the course of normal manuscript preparation.

GRAPHICS

Long before man learned to write he drew pictures on the walls of his cave. Now, with the advent of the home computer, he has an unlimited amount of wall space (CRT screen) and chalk (computer-controlled CRT electron beam). All he has in common with his ancestors is imagination and the will to create.

Several excellent graphics displays are available, most as peripherals for existing hobby computers, and with the proper programming can show almost anything the user desires on the screen. Some graphics display systems are made in full color—usually by using a color-TV set as the monitor. One complete color computer (Compucolor) is built as a system.

In most cases these display systems depend on programs that take advantage of the graphics and are written on paper tape, for those that have a tape reader, or on cassette tape, that most useful of interfaces. Once the programs are entered in the computer the operating instructions appear on screen as the program runs.

With just a little experience most hobbyists can devise their own programs for graphics. In one color peripheral (the Dazzler) programs allow the user to specify the colors and shapes and sometimes limited animation.

Some peripherals use "joysticks" to control the position of an electronic "target" that the computer draws on the monitor's CRT screen.

A joystick looks like a small metal "gear shift" arm that protrudes from a small box containing the electronics. The other end of the joystick (the one in the box) is mechanically connected to a pair of controls (potentiometers) arranged so that when the joystick is moved from side to side one of the controls is activated; when the joystick is moved back and forth, the other control operates. The two controls are electrically connected to an I/O port in the computer and each control moves an on-screen electronic "target" in the same direction as the joystick.

Two joysticks are needed when competitive games are played on screen; one player uses his joystick to "chase" the other. If only one participant is playing, he can thread his way through a maze with his joystick. Many programs are written for one, two, and even more joystick controls.

HOME COMPUTER NETWORKS

Although the hardware (modems) is currently available, there has not yet been any large-scale hobby-computer-to-hobby-computer communications, probably because of the relative lack of experience of most computer hobbyists.

There is no doubt, however, that in a year or so this means of communications will make its appearance, probably in a computer club as a "club newsletter" interchange. One central computer, belonging to one of the club members, will be fitted with a modem and its own telephone line. All the pertinent news for that week, such as meeting times and places, private messages, who has what for sale (flea market), and other items of interest will be placed in memory.

Club members can then phone into the club computer and connect their modems and computers on line. The two computers will pass data back and forth. In this way the "newsletter" can be kept up to date—within the hour if necessary. It will resemble a private telegraph system for club members.

This private network can also be used to pass software between individual members simply by placing a telephone call and having the two computers "talk" together. Thus any two members can pass along "computer things" such as software that could not be done in any other way except on tape or in writing.

ROBOTS

Until a few short years ago the idea of a self-contained robot was just a science-fiction dream. With the introduction of the low-cost microprocessor and semiconductor memory, however, the dream can be made a reality. Now, for the first time a serious robot creator has access to a reasonably priced "brain" and optical links between the robot and a "mother" computer. By taking advantage of the large number of I/O ports the on-board processor can "talk" to, he can create arms and fingers by the use of some relatively simple mechanics and low-power electric motors.

Essentially all the hardware required to build a robot is available at this time if you consult the catalogs of the surplus parts dealers who advertise in most electronics hobby magazines.

Figure 13.2 illustrates a concept that a couple of hobbyists are now considering. Some details are given for the reader's consideration.

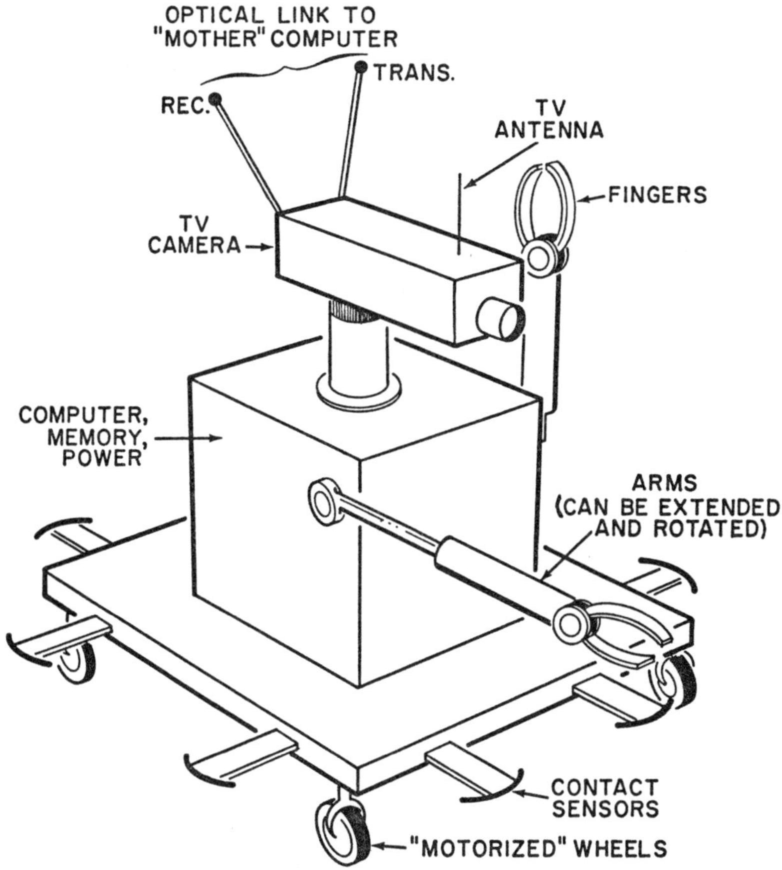

Figure 13.2 An example of a computer-controlled robot.

The robot is not "android" (human-looking) because we have not yet solved the vertical stability problem (gyroscopes and balance controllers). In time, this problem will be overcome. At present the robot moves around on motorized wheels which are built around a motor and revolve when power is applied. They are available from several sources (Edmund Scientific is one) and are powered by an on-board motorcycle battery. Control is exercised by one of the computer output ports.

The large "body" in the center mounts the computer, several K of semiconductor memory, and some ROMs. The ROMs contain the operating system and tell the on-board motors what to do whenever the computer becomes inoperative. Several contact sensors around the perimeter of the support base are used to signal the computer that the robot has met a solid object. This signal will cause the computer to move the robot away from that object. The on-board solid-state TV camera is mounted on a rotating platform to allow the camera to "look" around. The TV signal is sent via a small RF transmitter back to the operating base.

The two (or more) arms can be positioned at almost any angle and have an extension capability (unlike human arms). At the end of each arm is a set of fingers that can be closed around a small object for rotation or lifting. Strain sensors in each set of fingers allow them to pick up objects without crushing them.

The two antennas form an optical link between the robot and the mother computer, which also has a pair of antennas as its output port. The robot is then addressed by the computer as if it were just another terminal, but in this case an optical link (such as infrared diodes) is used in place of a hand-wired connection.

In operation the robot starts with its internal ROM program and leaves its "habitat" (where the wheel batteries are charged) and starts to wander around. If the room, or area, in which the robot will operate is always the same, the mother computer can talk to the robot and dump a program in the robot's memory for execution. The TV camera (optional) can be used to keep track of the robot at all times if the robot does not remain in visual range.

If an on-board gyroscope (with suitable pickoffs) and a wheel counter are used, it then becomes possible to program some very complex moves in the computer. The robot can then perform many operations.

The construction is not so complex as you might think. You will have to have some knowledge of mechanics so that the physical robot can operate as desired (this could be a group project with some people handling the mechanics, others, the control electronics). The computer people will handle both the computer and programming.

The wheels and their power are quite conventional and require only an electric switching circuit to start them, reverse them, and possibly rotate them to permit the robot to move sideways. The electric switching circuit is driven by the computer.

The contact sensors can be almost any small switches that are activated by pressure contacts, and all they need to do is stop the drive motors or initiate a robot turn around when outside contact in made. A signal will be sent to the mother computer at that time; otherwise the contact sensors need only control the drive motors.

The arms can use conventional stepping motors that rotate a fixed angular distance (either way) when they receive a computer-controlled pulse. The arms can be as complex as desired, and because most hobby computers can control as many as 256 output ports quite a number of stepping motors may be used to make some real complex "arm" movements.

Conclusion

By the time you get to this point you should have a pretty good idea of what personal computers are all about. You should know how humans and computers interact and be reasonably up to date on the available types of equipment. Now you can pick up any of the hobby computer magazines and be able to understand most of the articles and advertisements.

The only thing left is to continue your education in this area by reading specialized material on the subjects that interest you the most—whether hardware or software.

Drop into your local computer store and join your local computer club. Most of all start reading computer publications to add to your basic knowledge.

The once-closed door is now ajar . . . .

Appendixes

A. THE ABACUS
B. THE ALTAIR S-100 BUS
C. ASCII CODE
D. THE CARE AND FEEDING OF YOUR COMPUTER
E. WHAT DO YOU DO WHEN SOMETHING GOES WRONG?

APPENDIX A THE ABACUS

The abacus (Figure A.1) consists of a rectangular frame in which a series of counting bars or wires passes through a crossbar and affixes to the frame. One side of the crossbar has five beads in the "units" portion and two beads in the "fives" portion. Numbers are represented by placing the beads against the crossbar. Each of the two beads is worth five units of that section, whereas each of the five beads represents one unit. The number here is 836. The abacus shown is Chinese. The Japanese abacus (soroban) has only one bead above and four below the crossbar; operation is similar, however. Note that each column goes up by decade steps as you move to the left. The engraved dots on the crossbar are there to indicate decimal points.

Now, let's add 27 to the 836 for a total of 863. To add the 7 we start with the "units" section by dropping the last 5 bead to the bar and raising two of the "units" beads. Because we now have the two 5 beads at the bar, we can raise the pair to the frame (neutralizing them) and raise one of the unit "10 beads" to the three already there. This produces the total of 843.

We can now add the 2 to the "tens" position, but we have only one unit of 10 beads left. Once this bead is raised, we will have five units; therefore we can drop one of the 5s in the 10s column and then drop all the units beads to the frame. To add the last 10 raise one of the beads in the 10s column. The total is now 863.

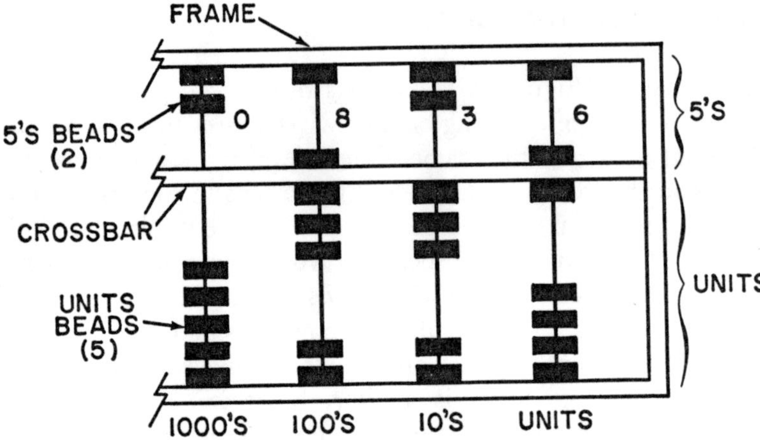

Figure A.1 The abacus.

APPENDIX B THE ALTAIR S-100 BUS

Pin	Signal	
1	+ 8 volts	power to PC boards
2	+ 16 volts	power to PC boards
3	XRDY	AND'ed with PRDY (pin 72) for 8080 RDY
4	VIØ	vector interrupt request Ø
5	VI1	" " " 1
6	VI2	" " " 2
7	VI3	" " " 3
8	VI4	" " " 4
9	VI5	" " " 5
10	VI6	" " " 6
11	VI7	" " " 7
12	XRDY2	additional ready for CPU
13		
14		
15		still undefined
16		
17		
18	$\overline{\text{STA DSB}}$	status buffer disable
19	$\overline{\text{C/C DSB}}$	command/control buffer disable
20	UNPROT	input to memory protect circuits on memory boards
21	SS	computer in single-step mode
22	$\overline{\text{ADD DSB}}$	address buffer disable
23	$\overline{\text{DO DSB}}$	data out (from CPU) buffer disable
24	Ø2	phase two clock signal
25	Ø1	phase one clock
26	PHLDA	hold acknowledge, buffered 8080 output

27	PWAIT	wait acknowledge, buffered 8080 output
28	PINTE	interrupt enable, buffered 8080 output
29	A5	address line 5
30	A4	address line 4
31	A3	address line 3
32	A15	address line 15
33	A12	address line 12
34	A9	address line 9
35	DO1	data out line 1
36	DOØ	data out line 0
37	A10	address line 10
38	DO4	data out line 4
39	DO5	data out line 5
40	DO6	data out line 6
41	DI2	data input line 2
42	DI3	data input line 3
43	DI7	data input line 7
44	SM1	latched 8080 M1 status
45	SOUT	latched 8080 OUT status
46	SINP	latched 8080 INP status
47	SMEMR	latched 8080 MEMR status
48	SHLTA	latched 8080 HALT status
49	CLOCK	2-MHz clock
50	GND	system ground
51 (A)	+ 8 volts	power to PC boards
52 (B)	– 16 volts	power to board negative regulators
53 (C)	$\overline{\text{SSW DSB}}$	sense switch disable
54 (D)	$\overline{\text{EXT CLR}}$	clear signal for I/O devices
55 (E)	RTC	60-Hz for real-time clock
56 (F)	$\overline{\text{STS TB}}$	strobe signal to allow status signals

Pin	Signal	Description
		to be set
57 (H)	DIGI	enables CPU data input drivers
58 (J)	FRDY	used by display/control logic
59 (K)		
60 (L)		
61 (M)		
62 (N)		
63 (P)		undefined at present
64 (R)		
65 (S)		
66 (T)		
67 (U)		
68 (V)	MWRT	write enable signal for memory
69 (W)	$\overline{\text{PS}}$	indicates if addressed memory is protected
70 (X)	PROT	input to memory protect circuits
71 (Y)	RUN	indicates computer is in run mode
72 (Z)	PRDY	AND'ed with XRDY (pin 3) and goes to 8080 RDY
73 (a)	$\overline{\text{PINT}}$	input to 8080 interrupt request
74 (b)	$\overline{\text{PHOLD}}$	input to 8080 hold request
75 (c)	$\overline{\text{PRESET}}$	clear signal for CPU
76 (d)	$\overline{\text{PSYNC}}$	buffered 8080 sync signal
77 (e)	$\overline{\text{PWR}}$	buffered 8080 write enable signal
78 (f)	PDBIN	buffered 8080 PDBIN signal
79 (h)	AØ	address line 0
80 (j)	A1	address line 1
81 (k)	A2	address line 2
82 (l)	A6	address line 6
83 (m)	A7	address line 7
84 (n)	A8	address line 8
85 (p)	A13	address line 13
86 (r)	A14	address line 14

87 (s)	A11	address line 11
88 (t)	DO2	data out line 2
89 (u)	DO3	data out line 3
90 (v)	DO7	data out line 7
91 (w)	DI4	data input line 4
92 (x)	DI5	data input line 5
93 (y)	DI6	data input line 6
94 (z)	DI1	data input line 1
95 (AA)	DIØ	data input line 0
96 (AB)	SINTA	latched 8080 INTA status
97 (AC)	$\overline{\text{SWO}}$	latched 8080 WO status
98 (AD)	SSTACK	latched 8080 STACK status
99 (AE)	$\overline{\text{POC}}$	clear signal during power up
100 (AF)	GND	system ground

Figure A-2

The Altair (S-100) bus. The small line found above certain entries is called a vinculum and means "not."

APPENDIX C ASCII CODE

ASCII, American Standard Code for Information Interchange, is the official "language" of computers and terminals. Whereas humans use a complex method of communication, a computer understands only "machine language." To establish a man-machine exchange, some way must be found to "translate" instructions. When the operator depresses the A key on his keyboard, the internal mechanism translates it into a machine-language (1s and 0s) code; for example, in the case of the letter A, 41; in the case of a ?, 3F.

Now translate in the opposite direction. If you were writing a machine-language program and you wanted the computer to print the number 2, you would have to instruct the machine to print 32. The ASCII table shown here is in hexidecimal, but it can be converted to octal.

The mysterious letter codes in the two left rows are machine instructions (explained below) that are not printed by the readout but are used to tell the machine what operations to perform.

Second Hex Character	First Hex Character 0	1	2	3	4	5	6	7
0	NUL	DLE	SP	0	@	P	\	p
1	SOH	DC1	!	1	A	Q	a	q
2	STX	DC2	“	2	B	R	b	r
3	ETX	DC3	#	3	C	S	c	s
4	EOT	DC4	$	4	D	T	d	t
5	ENQ	NAK	%	5	E	U	e	u
6	ACK	SYN	&	6	F	V	f	v
7	BEL	ETB	’	7	G	W	g	w
8	BS	CAN	(	8	H	X	h	x
9	HT	EM	)	9	I	Y	i	y
A	LF	SUB	*	:	J	Z	j	z
B	VT	ESC	+	;	K	[	k	{
C	FF	FS	,	<	L	\	l	|
D	CR	GS	–	=	M	]	m	}
E	SO	RS	.	>	N	^	n	~
F	SI	US	/	?	O	-	o	DEL

Figure A-3 ASCII Code

Abbreviations

SOH	Start of heading	DC2	Device Control 2
STX	Start of text	DC3	Device Control 3
ETX	End of text	DC4	Device Control 4
EOT	End of transmission	NAK	Negative acknowledge
ENQ	Enquiry	SYN	Synchronous idle
ACK	Acknowledge	ETB	End of transmission block
BEL	Bell or alarm	CAN	Cancel
BS	Backspace	EM	End of medium
HT	Horizontal tabulation	SUB	Substitute
LF	Line feed	ESC	Escape
VT	Vertical tabulation	FS	File separator
FF	Form feed	GS	Group separator
CR	Carriage return	RS	Record separator
SO	Shift out	US	Unit separator
SI	Shift in	SP	Space
DLE	Data link escape	DEL	Delete
DC1	Device control 1		

APPENDIX D THE CARE AND FEEDING OF YOUR OWN COMPUTER

A hobby computer represents a sizable investment in cash, similar to that made in a high-quality hi-fi system, a ham installation, or a photo lab, and quite a bit of care is required to protect it.

First decide on the location. A computer with its associated keyboard, CRT monitor, and so on, should be installed in some out-of-the-traffic-pattern area in your house or apartment. The installation must be as permanent as possible. The area should have adequate electric power and be reasonably well ventilated. Make sure that you also have sufficient storage space for magazines, computer documentation, cassettes, and other equipment.

A kitchen-style table, large enough to support the computer and its peripherals, plus room to spread magazines, schematics, and notepaper, should be provided. Seating should be comfortable, preferably with more than one chair; computer hobbyists tend to cluster at one another's installation.

The power to the computer table should be controlled by one central master switch in order that the entire system may be shut down. Otherwise you may find that something was left running all night because it didn't have a pilot lamp. Switch-controlled multioutlet power strips can be bought at most electrical stores.

Some hobbyists prefer to mount their computers and CRT monitors on shelves above the operating table. This arrangement allows more room for writing, reference to documentation, or simply opening large schematics.

Eating and drinking around a computer system should be done with great care. It doesn't take many crumbs under a key to make that key inactive and ants in the bus system are to be avoided! Beware also of the dreaded "Coke plague" which results from spilled sugary soft drinks (or beer) and can form all manner of strange growths (some conducting) inside a complex piece of electronic equipment.

If you do any metalworking or soldering or any messing around with metals at all, make sure that protective covers are on all pieces of equipment. It is amazing how minute pieces of metal find their way into densely packed printed circuit boards or inside multipin connectors to cause all kinds of trouble.

If your equipment is not protected, buy suitable covers or make your own of plastic. Keep in mind that an ounce of prevention is worth a hundred hours of troubleshooting and discovering that a small piece of wire you cut off yesterday and that somehow disappeared is the culprit.

Because the noisiest part of most computers is the relatively quiet ventilation fan (unless you have a Teletype), an operating system running at full blast will not arouse sleeping children nor disturb the next-door neighbors. It is only in sci-fi movies that computers make those strange unearthly noises!

One of the handiest things to have around, in the way of mass storage, is a cassette, disk, or what-have-you that contains several computer games—preferably card-type games, for almost all are well known to adults—and a couple of children's games. These are always nice to have around when visiting friends or neighbors ask that inevitable question: what do you do with a computer? Once adults have tried to beat the computer at some card game or have tried not to crash a Lunar Lander, they know. If children bother you, keep them at bay with simpler programs. It is amazing how many children have been kept out of adults' hair with "Hurkle" and similar games. Your major problem will be keeping those friends and neighbors away from your computer!

APPENDIX E WHAT DO YOU DO WHEN SOMETHING GOES WRONG?

This is a difficult question to answer, for it all depends on your level of software and hardware experience and the test equipment you have at your disposal. Obviously, if you have the experience, you will know where to start your search and how to look.

If, however, you are still in the learning stages, there are several things you can do beyond taking a fire axe to the computer!

One is to go to the computer store where you bought the original piece of equipment. These specialized stores normally have the trained help and the repair facilities to put everything back in order. Their prices in most cases are reasonable and you can discuss your problem with the technician who repaired the faulty item to find out why it failed and how you can prevent a recurrence. Computer-store services are also time and money savers compared with sending the faulty item back to the original kit (or peripheral) manufacturer for overhaul. Manufacturers in general are busy and the repair may take some time. Don't forget the mail time both ways, plus the additional cost of shipping and insurance.

Then there is your computer club (every computer hobbyist should belong to a computer club!). In almost every club there is usually one other person who will have the same piece of equipment up and running in his computer. The two of you can easily make voltage and waveform comparisons to determine what is wrong with your device; and just about every computer club has a couple of hardware "hot shots" who take great pleasure in whipping a problem. These fellows generally have all the necessary test equipment to do the job.

So, after the initial panic has worn off, start making your calls. Keep in mind that there is always a good possibility that the peripheral that failed did not fail electronically and that the mysterious software phantom has struck again!

Glossary

address the digital value that reveals the location of a device in the memory

alphanumerics the digits 0 through 9, the letters of the alphabet, and certain punctuation marks

ASCII acronym for American Standard Code for Information Interchange

assembler a computer program that translates a symbolic program into machine language

A to D converter analog to digital converter used to change proportional electric signals to digital form

backplane a circuit board mounting connectors into which computer circuits are plugged; the interconnection between circuit boards is made by the printed or wire-wrapped connection on the backplane

base a property of a number system

BASIC short for Beginner's All-purpose Symbolic Instruction Code; the most common high-level language used by computer hobbyists

baud a unit of signaling speed in bits per second

BAUDOT code a 5-bit character code used in older Teletypes and still used for radio Teletype communications

benchmark a test problem used to compare computers; criteria may be speed, ease of programming, and over all cost

binary number system with only two digits, 0 and 1

bit *b*inary-dig*it;* one piece of digital information; 8 make 1 byte

bootstrap a machine routine that tells the computer where to look for data and what to do with it

bug a hardware or software defect

bus one or more conductors that distribute data, control signals, and power in a computer

byte a generic term that represents the number of bits used, ordinarily eight

cassette a plastic holder that contains a length of magnetic tape on which to store programs; the same device is used in low-cost audio recording

chip the name given to an integrated circuit (IC)

clock the basic electric synchronizing signal in a computer

computer a system capable of accepting data, processing it, and delivering an appropriate output; a computer consists of input and output devices, storage, arithmetic, logical, and control units

CPU abbreviation for central processing unit

CRT abbreviation for cathode ray tube

CURSOR on a CRT-type display block underline, or overline that points out the position of the next character

data a general term used to describe facts or concepts in a formalized manner suitable for processing by a computer

debugging the detection, location, and removal of hardware or software malfunctions in a computing system

decimal a number represented in the base-10 number system

DIP abbreviation for dual in-line package, the plastic case of an IC

documentation all of the written information required to create, test, and maintain system hardware or software

DOS *d*isk *o*perating *s*ystem, a program that causes a disk storage system to store or retrieve data

edit arrange data for reasonableness and proper range, to make sure that it can be used by a computer

EPROM an erasable programmable read only memory (see also ROM, PROM)

EXECUTE to perform the sequence of operations specified by the computer program

FETCH a portion of the computer cycle in which data are obtained from a storage location

file an organized collection of related data

flip-flop an electronic circuit that has two opposite polarity outputs that are interchanged by an electronic clock signal

flowchart a graphical representation for the solution of a problem

graphics in electronics usually applied to a CRT terminal which can display pictures in various forms

hard copy printed output of the computer data

handshaking control signals that allow two electronic circuits to synchronize their operations

hardware the physical elements of a computer (in contrast to software)

hexidecimal a number system based on the base 16 number system

high-level language a computer programming scheme that is independent of the computer being used; the most common high-level language is BASIC

IC abbreviation for integrated circuit

Input/Output usually abbreviated I/O; a general term for a peripheral that enables the computer to communicate with the outside world

instruction a program step that tells the computer what to do for a single step in a program

instruction a set of characters that defines a basic computer operation

interface the boundary between two pieces of hardware or between two systems

JUMP a software instruction that causes the computer to go to a particular sequence of operations

k abbreviation for thousand (kilo)

kit a group of discrete components that can be assembled to form a complete system

language a defined set of symbols and rules for combination in meaningful communications

LED abbreviation for light-emitting diode, a semiconductor junction that when energized emits a red, green, or yellow glow, depending on the chemical construction

logic circuit a network of logical elements that performs a specified function

machine language the fundamental "language" of a computer, written as a group of l's and 0's

memory the storage facility in a computer

microprocessor the "brain" of a microcomputer system; contains the arithmetic unit and special register groups

microsecond one-millionth of a second

mother board a large-sized printed circuit board that can support a number of "plug-in" boards

MPU abbreviation for microprocessing unit (see CPU, microprocessor)

nanosecond one-billionth of a second

octal a number system based on the base 8 number system that includes only the digits 0 through 7

operating system a software package that enables the user to communicate with a computer

parallel simultaneous processing of all the elements in a data group

patch software coding inserted in a routine to correct a mistake or to alter a routine

peripheral any of a number of optional devices that can be used with a microcomputer

pin out the identification of each pin of an integrated circuit by number and signal

plug in a peripheral device that can be inserted in a computer bus structure via a connector on the bus

port a channel through which data can enter or leave a computer

printer an electromechanical device that accepts computer data and produces hard copy

printed circuit a plastic sheet with an electronic circuit formed by copper traces between pertinent connections

program the instructions required to solve a particular problem on a computer

PROM a programmable read only memory (see also ROM, EPROM)

prompter a nonalphanumeric term used to indicate that the computer operating system is waiting for instructions

RAM abbreviation for random access memory, used by the computer to store data

register temporary storage location in a processor

ROM abbreviation for read only memory

routine a sequence of machine instructions to carry out a defined function

software programs that cause the computer to carry out a particular operation

serial handling data one bit at a time

subroutine a set of instructions that carries out a defined operation; may be used many times during a program

tape strip of material that my be punched (paper tape) or coated with magnetic material (cassette tape)

Teletype trademark of the Teletype Corporation; a device that includes a keyboard (optional tape reader) for originating messages and a hard-copy printer (or tape perforator) for accepting them

terminal an input/output device coupled to a computer

three-state a special logic circuit that can be electrically isolated from its bus

video a TV-like electric signal consisting of horizontal and vertical sync and associated line-brightness components

volatile the characteristic of becoming lost or erased when power is removed (as data in a RAM)

word an ordered set of characters that is treated by the computer as a single unit; for example, 8 bits make 1 byte, usually called a word

Index